THE

DHARMA FLOWER

SUTRA

CHE
WONDERFUL DHARMA
LOCUS FLOWER
SUCRA

Translated into Chinese by
Tripitaka Master Kumarajiva of Yao Ch'in

Volume 9
Chapter 10: Masters of the Dharma
Chapter 11: Vision of the Jeweled Stupa

with the commentary of
CRIPICAKA
MASCER hUA

Translated into English by
The Buddhist Text Translation Society
San Francisco
1981

Translated by the Buddhist Text Translation Society

Primary translation: Bhikshuni Heng-yin
Reviewed by: Bhikshuni Heng-ch'ih
Edited by: Upasika Kuo-lin Lethcoe

Certified by: The Venerable Master Hua

Printed in the United States of America

First printing-- 1981

For information address:
      Sino American Buddhist Association
      Dharma Realm Buddhist University
      Gold Mountain Monastery
      1731 15th Street
      San Francisco, California 94103
      U.S.A.
      (415) 621-5202
      (415) 861-9672

ISBN 0-917512-85-5

Acknowledgements:

Cover: Bhikshuni Heng-chieh
Index: Bhikshuni Heng-ming
English calligraphy (Sutra text and other) Jerri-jo
Illuminated letters: Kuo-ling Pecaites
Graphics and layout: Jerri-jo Idarius and
   Kuo-ling Pecaites
Photo of the Master: Kuo-ying Brevoort
Commentary typed by: Upasika Kuo-shan

TABLE OF CONTENTS

Buddhist Text Translation Society
Eight Regulations

A translator must free himself or herself from the motives of personal fame and reputation.

A translator must cultivate an attitude free from arrogance and conceit.

A translator must refrain from aggrandizing himself or herself and denigrating others.

A translator must not establish himself or herself as the standard of correctness and suppress the work of others with his or her faultfinding.

A translator must take the Buddha-mind as his or her own mind.

A translator must use the wisdom of the Selective Dharma Eye to determine true principles.

A translator must request the Elder Virtuous Ones of the ten directions to certify his or her translations.

A translator must endeavor to propagate the teachings by printing sutras, shastra texts, and vinaya texts when the translations are certified as being correct.

TRIPITAKA
MASTER HUA

OUTLINE: CHAPTER TEN

C3. Section of Propagation (1543)
D1. Dharma Master Chapter
  E1. Praising upholders of the Dharma
    F1. Showing disciples deep merit and blessings of those who
        uphold the Dharma
      G1. Disciples during the Buddha's time
      G2. Disciples after the Buddha's extinction (1544)
    F2. Showing catergories of disciples (1546)
      G1. Prose
        H1. Specific explanation
          I1. Present
            J1. Lower classification of masters
            J2. Higher class of masters (1548)
          I2. Future (1550)
            J1. Lower class of masters
            J2. Higher class of masters (1551)
        H2. General explanation (1553)
      G2. Verse (1557)
        H1. Exhortation to self-practice and benefitting others
        H2. Repetition of specific and general meanings (1566)
          I1. Verse of specific explanation
            J1. Present
            J2. Future (1571)
          I2. Verse of general explanation (1575)
        H3. Conclusion: praising the Sutra as foremost (1581)
  E2. Praising the Dharma maintained and showing method of propagation (1588)
    F1. Prose
      G1. Praising the Sutra-dharma
        H1. Praising the Dharma

H1. Searching for the person
H2. Three Buddhas' exhortation to hold the Sutra (1763)
H3. Shakyamuni Buddha's exhortation (1764)
G2. Difficulty of upholding Dharma and exhortation to propagate it (1766)
    H1. Exhorting
        I1. Sincere exhortation
        I2. Difficulty of upholding this Sutra (1770)
        I3. Explaining the difficulty of upholding the Sutra (1776)
    H2. Shakyamuni Buddha's exhortation (1777)
        I1. Searching for the person
        I2. Showing how the Buddhas rejoice when one can uphold that which is difficult to uphold (1778)
        I3. The accomplishment of one's own practice and teaching others (1780)

Chapter Ten
Masters of the Dharma

There are five types of Dharma masters. The first is the Dharma Master who receives and holds (the teaching). He receives the Dharma into his mind and he understands the Dharma with his person. With his mind he understands the Dharma, and with his body he puts the Dharma into actual practice. The second type of Dharma Master is one who reads the texts. The third type of Dharma Master recites the texts from memory. The fourth type of Dharma Master copies out the Sutras. The fifth type of Dharma Master explains the Sutras to others, lectures on the Sutras and explains their meaning.

The first four types of Dharma Masters practice self benefit. The fifth type practices benefitting others; they teach and transform other people. When you receive and uphold the Sutras, read, recite and copy them out, you are benefitting yourself. To explain the Sutras to others is to benefit them.

A Dharma Master is defined as "one who takes the Dharma as Master." One takes the Buddhadharma as one's teacher. A Dharma Master is also defined as "one who bestows the Dharma on others." In this chapter, Dharma Masters receive predictions from the Buddha and so this is titled MASTERS OF THE DHARMA.

Sutra = T. 262, 30b29

At that time the World Honored One, through Medicine King Bodhisattva, spoke to the eighty thousand great lords saying, "Medicine King, do you see within this great assembly the limitless gods, dragon kings, yakshas, gandharvas, asuras, garudas, kinnaras, mahoragas, and beings both human and non human, as well as the Bhikshus, Bhikshunis, Upasakas, Upasikas, those seeking to be Sound Hearers, those seeking to be Pratyekabuddhas, and those seeking the Buddha Path? Upon such ones as these, all in the presence of the Buddha, who hear but one verse or one *sentence of The Wonderful Dharma Lotus Flower Sutra, or who have even one thought of rejoicing in it, I bestow predictions of their future attainment of Anuttarasamyaksambodhi."*

Outline:

    C3. Section of propagation.
      D1. Dharma Master Chapter.
        E1. Praising those who uphold the Dharma.
          F1. Showing the disciples deep merit and the
            blessings of those who uphold the Dharma.
            G1. Disciples during the Buddha's time.

Commentary:

AT THAT TIME, THE WORLD HONORED ONE, Shakyamuni Buddha, THROUGH MEDICINE KING BODHISATTVA, SPOKE TO THE EIGHTY THOUSAND GREAT LORDS, Great Bodhisattvas, SAYING, "MEDICINE KING Bodhisattva, DO YOU SEE WITHIN THIS GREAT ASSEMBLY THE LIMITLESS GODS, DRAGON KINGS, YAKSHAS, the speedy ghosts who fly through space, GHANDHARVAS, the musical spirits in the court of the Jade Emperor, ASURAS, GARUDAS, the golden winged p'eng birds. KINNARAS, another class of musical spirit in the Jade Emperor's Court. MAHORAGAS, the big snakes, AND BEINGS BOTH HUMAN AND NON HUMAN, AS WELL AS THE BHIKSHUS, BHIKSHUNIS, UPASAKAS, UPASIKAS, THOSE SEEKING TO BE SOUND HEARERS, THOSE SEEKING TO BE PRATYEKABUDDHAS, AND THOSE SEEKING THE BUDDHA PATH? UPON SUCH ONES AS THESE, ALL IN THE PRESENCE OF THE BUDDHA, WHO HEAR BUT ONE VERSE OR ONE SENTENCE OF THE WONDERFUL DHARMA LOTUS FLOWER SUTRA, OR

1544

WHO HAVE EVEN ONE THOUGHT OF REJOICING IN IT, I BESTOW
PREDICTIONS OF THEIR FUTURE ATTAINMENT OF ANUTTARASAMYAK-
SAMBODHI. They shall all obtain the unsurpassed
enlightenment, the position of Buddhahood.

Sutra: T. 30 c7

*The Buddha told Medicine King: "Further-
more, after the extinction of the Thus Come One,
should there be one who hears but a single verse
or a single sentence of The Wonderful Dharma
Lotus Flower Sutra or who has even one thought
of rejoicing in it, I bestow upon him as well a
prediction of Anuttarasamyaksambodhi.*

Outline:

> G2. Disciples after the Buddha's
> extinction.

Commentary:

THE BUDDHA TOLD MEDICINE KING: "FURTHERMORE, AFTER
THE EXTINCTION OF THE THUS COME ONE, after the Buddha
has entered Nirvana, SHOULD THERE BE ONE WHO HEARS BUT A
SINGLE VERSE OR A SINGLE SENTENCE OF THE WONDERFUL DHARMA
LOTUS FLOWER SUTRA, OR WHO HAS EVEN ONE THOUGHT OF
REJOICING IN IT, but one thought of rejoicing." "Rejoic-
ing" includes praising the sutra, receiving and upholding
it, reading and reciting it, writing it out as well." I
BESTOW UPON HIM AS WELL A PREDICTION OF ANUTTARASAMYAK-
SAMBODHI."

Sutra: T. 30c9

"Further, should there be one who receives and upholds, reads and recites, explains and teaches, or copies out The Wonderful Dharma Lotus Flower Sutra, be it even a single verse, looking upon the sutra text with reverence as he would the Buddha himself, making various kinds of offerings of flowers, incense, beads, powdered incense, paste incense, burning incense, silk canopies, banners, clothing and music, or who even join his palms in reverence, O Medicine King, you should know that such a person has in the past already made offerings to tens of myriads of millions of Buddhas, in the presence of those Buddhas, accomplishing great vows. It is out of pity for living beings that he is born among human beings.

"O Medicine King, if someone should ask you what type of living beings shall in the future become Buddhas, you should point out to him that these very people in the future certainly shall become Buddhas. Why is this? If a good man or good woman receives and upholds, reads, recites, explains and teaches, or writes out even a single *sentence of The Wonderful Dharma Lotus Flower Sutra, or makes various offerings to the sutra text of flowers, incense, beads, powdered incense, paste incense, burning incense, silk canopies, banners, clothing, music, or reverently joined palms, that person should be looked up to in reverence by those in all worlds and should receive offerings befitting the Thus Come One. You should know that this person is a great Bodhisattva, one who has accomplished Anuttarasamyaksambodhi. Out of pity for living beings, he has vowed to be born here and to expound upon The Wonderful Dharma Lotus Flower Sutra broadly and in detail.*

Outline:

> F2. Showing categories of disciples.
> > G1. Prose.
> > > H1. Specific explanation.
> > > > I1. Present.
> > > > > J1. Lower classification of masters.

Commentary:

"FURTHER, SHOULD THERE BE ONE WHO RECEIVES AND UP-HOLDS, READS AND RECITES, EXPLAINS AND TEACHES, OR COPIES OUT THE WONDERFUL DHARMA LOTUS FLOWER SUTRA, BE IT EVEN A SINGLE VERSE, LOOKING UPON THE SUTRA TEXT WITH REVER-ENCE AS HE WOULD THE BUDDHA HIMSELF, MAKING VARIOUS KINDS

OF OFFERINGS OF FLOWERS, INCENSE, BEADS, POWDERED INCENSE, PASTE INCENSE, BURNING INCENSE, SILK CANOPIES, BANNERS, CLOTHING AND MUSIC singing praises, OR WHO EVEN JOINS HIS PALMS IN REVERENCE, O MEDICINE KING, YOU SHOULD KNOW THAT SUCH A PERSON HAS IN THE PAST MADE OFFERINGS TO TENS OF MYRIADS OF MILLIONS OF BUDDHAS, IN THE PRESENCE OF THOSE BUDDHAS, ACCOMPLISHING GREAT VOWS. IT IS OUT OF PITY FOR LIVING BEINGS, these Bodhisattva Dharma Masters have compassion for living beings, THAT HE IS BORN AMONG HUMAN BEINGS.

"O MEDICINE KING, IF SOMEONE SHOULD ASK YOU WHAT TYPE OF LIVING BEINGS SHALL IN THE FUTURE BECOME BUDDHAS, YOU SHOULD POINT OUT TO HIM THAT THESE VERY PEOPLE IN THE FUTURE CERTAINLY SHALL BECOME BUDDHAS. Those Dharma Masters who receive and uphold, copy out, read and recite, and explain the Sutra to others, or those who hear but a single sentence or verse of The Lotus Sutra--these people will become Buddhas. WHY IS THIS? IF A GOOD MAN OR GOOD WOMAN RECEIVES, UPHOLDS, READS, RECITES, EXPLAINS AND TEACHES OR WRITES OUT EVEN A SINGLE SENTENCE OF THE WONDERFUL DHARMA LOTUS FLOWER SUTRA, OR   MAKES VARIOUS OFFERINGS TO THE SUTRA TEXT OF FLOWERS, INCENSE, BEADS, POWDERED INCENSE, PASTE INCENSE, BURNING INCENSE, SILK CANOPIES, BANNERS, CLOTHING, MUSIC, OR REVERENTLY JOINED PALMS...Why should one make offerings to the Sutras? It's because the Sutras are just the Dharma body of the Buddha. THAT PERSON SHOULD BE LOOKED UP TO IN REVERENCE

BY THOSE IN ALL WORLDS AND SHOULD RECEIVE OFFERINGS
BEFITTING THE THUS COME ONE. You should make offerings
to these Dharma Masters as you would make offerings to
the Buddha. YOU SHOULD KNOW THAT THIS PERSON IS A GREAT
BODHISATTVA...Those who lecture upon The Dharma Flower
Sutra after the Buddha's extinction are great Bodhisattvas.
One WHO HAS ACCOMPLISHED ANUTTARASAMYAKSAMBODHI. Why
did he come into this world? OUT OF PITY FOR LIVING
BEINGS HE HAS VOWED TO BE BORN HERE AND TO EXPOUND UPON
THE WONDERFUL DHARMA FLOWER SUTRA BROADLY AND IN DETAIL.

Sutra: T. 30 c 23

"How much the more does this apply to one who can receive and uphold it in its entirety and make various kinds of offerings to it.

"Medicine King, you should know that this person has renounced his own pure karmic reward and, after my extinction, out of pity for living beings, has been born in the evil world to vastly proclaim this sutra.

Outline: J2. Praising the higher class of masters
Commentary:

"HOW MUCH THE MORE DOES THIS APPLY TO ONE WHO CAN
RECEIVE AND UPHOLD IT IN ITS ENTIRETY AND MAKE VARIOUS
KINDS OF OFFERINGS TO IT.

"MEDICINE KING, YOU SHOULD KNOW THAT THIS PERSON HAS

RENOUNCED HIS OWN PURE KARMIC REWARD AND, having already attained anuttarasamyaksambodhi, AFTER MY EXTINCTION, OUT OF PITY FOR LIVING BEINGS, HAS BEEN BORN IN THE EVIL WORLD of the five turbidities TO VASTLY PROCLAIM THIS SUTRA. This Dharma Master, after I enter Nirvana, will take pity on living beings and be reborn in the realm of the five turbidities to propagate The Lotus Sutra. So if you study The Dharma Flower Sutra and learn how to explain it to others, you don't have to ask to know that you are a Bodhisattva who has returned to save living beings. If this were not the case you would have no opportunity to meet up with The Dharma Flower Sutra, or, if you did have the chance to meet up with it, you surely wouldn't be able to explain it to other people. If you lecture The Dharma Flower Sutra, several thousands of years ago Shakyamuni Buddha already gave you a prediction. We who are investigating the Sutras now should each take one of them and investigate it in great detail until you understand it very well. Penetrate its meaning from beginning to end. Then you will be able to explain it, because you will have some foundation in the Buddhadharma. It's not enough just to listen to the Sutras being lectured. You must really understand their meaning well enough to explain them to others. Otherwise you are just wasting your time. Pick a Sutra you like and really get into it so that you understand it completely. Then that counts for something.

1550

Sutra: T. 30 c 26

*"If this good man or good woman after my
extinction can secretly explain even so much
as a single sentence of The Dharma Flower
Sutra for a single person, you should know
that this person is a messenger of the Thus
Come One, sent by the Thus Come One to do
the Thus Come One's work.*

Outline:

I2. Future.
J1. Lower class of Masters.

Commentary:

IF THIS GOOD MAN OR GOOD WOMAN, should it be the
case, that AFTER MY EXTINCTION CAN SECRETLY EXPLAIN EVEN
SO MUCH AS A SINGLE SENTENCE OF THE DHARMA FLOWER SUTRA
FOR A SINGLE PERSON..."Secretly" means not openly.
Perhaps the person doesn't dare lecture to groups of
people because he has stage fright. So he secretly explains the Sutra to just one person. Perhaps he's afraid
people will ask him questions he can't answer. Let's
say he doesn't even lecture the whole Sutra, but just a
single sentence. Which sentence? It doesn't matter.
Any sentence will do. YOU SHOULD KNOW THAT THIS PERSON
IS A MESSENGER OF THE THUS COME ONE, the Buddha sent him,
SENT BY THE THUS COME ONE to the world to explain The

Lotus Sutra, TO DO THE THUS COME ONE'S WORK. Lecturing
on The Dharma Flower Sutra is just doing the Buddha's
work. The Buddha's work is just The Dharma Flower Sutra.

Sutra: T. 30 c 28
*"How much the more so is this the case for
one who can in the midst of a great assembly
extensively explain it to people.*

Outline:

J2. Higher class of Masters

Commentary:

HOW MUCH THE MORE SO IS THIS THE CASE FOR ONE WHO
CAN, IN THE MIDST OF A GREAT ASSEMBLY, EXTENSIVELY EXPLAIN
IT TO PEOPLE. Any of you who can study The Dharma Flower
Sutra, understand it and then explain it for a gathering
of people, will be praised by the Buddha.

You say, "Well, Dharma Master, you're up there
lecturing it for us right now. Is the Thus Come One
praising you?"

Not only is he praising me now, but he did so in the
past and he will do so in the future. That's why I like
to lecture it so much! If the Thus Come One didn't praise
this activity, I wouldn't be undertaking it. I like
praise!! Hah!

In the past I used to lecture on The Dharma Flower

Sutra all the time, I also always used to go to lectures and listen. No matter what was going on, I always liked to lecture and listen.

Sutra : T. 30 c 29

"O Medicine King, should an evil person with unwholesome mind appear before the Buddha, slandering and scolding him constantly for the length of an aeon, his offenses would be relatively light compared to the offenses of a person who speaks even a single evil word reviling one who reads or recites The Dharma Flower Sutra. That person's offense would be very grave.

"O Medicine King, you should know that one who reads and recites The Dharma Flower Sutra takes the Buddha's adornments as his own adornments. He shall carry the Thus Come One on his shoulders. Wherever he goes, he should be welcomed with obeisance. Single-mindedly, and with palms joined, one should pay reverence, make offerings, honor, and praise him. He should receive the finest offerings among people, offerings of flowers, incense, beads, powdered incense, paste incense, burning *incense, silk canopies, banners, clothing, fine food, and music. Heavenly jewels should be scattered over him, and clusters of the finest heavenly jewels offered to him.*

"What is the reason? When this person joyfully speaks the Dharma, those who hear it for but an instant shall directly achieve ultimate Anuttarasamyaksambodhi."

Outline:

H2.   General explanation.

Commentary:

"O MEDICINE KING, SHOULD AN EVIL PERSON." How evil is this person? Not only does he scold his teacher, he even scolds the Buddha! Would you say he was evil or not? "WITH UNWHOLESOME MIND, evil mind, APPEAR BEFORE THE BUDDHA, SLANDERING AND SCOLDING HIM CONSTANTLY FOR THE LENGTH OF AN AEON." Let's just say it's a small aeon, that is 139,600 years. This is like Devadatta who always scolded the Buddha. As a result, he fell, alive into hell. "HIS OFFENSES WOULD BE RELATIVELY LIGHT." You should't think this phrase means that scolding the Buddha brings only light offenses. It only means that the offense is lighter than the offense of slandering one who recites The Dharma Flower Sutra. COMPARED TO THE OFFENSES OF A PERSON WHO SPEAKS EVEN A SINGLE EVIL

WORD REVILING ONE WHO READS OR RECITES THE DHARMA FLOWER SUTRA. Be they at-home or left-home, THAT PERSON'S OFFENSE WOULD BE VERY GRAVE." They say things about the reciter of The Dharma Flower Sutra, things like, "He recites The Dharma Flower Sutra? Are you kidding? He kills, steals, fools around, and drinks and everything!" It doesn't matter whether the one who recites is a left home person or a lay person.

As to receiving and upholding the Sutra, some do it outwardly and some do it inwardly. "Inwardly" means that it is done in secret. This is like Rahula who was first in secret practices. He recited Sutras and mantras but nobody knew. He didn't run up in front of everyone holding a copy of the Sutra and making a display of himself, "See me? I am upholding The Dharma Flower Sutra!!" To uphold it inwardly means that, silently, at all times, one is cultivating, and people don't necessarily know.

The same applies to reading and reciting. Rahula recited whether there were people there or not. Some people in Buddhism exclusively cheat people. If they see someone coming, they pick up a Sutra and start reciting like crazy. When the person leaves, they put it down and forget it. They just do it for show. Some people do the same thing with bowing to the Buddha, writing out Sutras, etc. Those who truly write out the Sutras do so whether anyone is there to watch them or not. A Dharma Master in Hong Kong was like this. When he wrote out the Sutra he always sat in full lotus and wrote it out with utmost respect in every word and every brush stroke. He had extremely fine handwriting, too.

The person who slanders one who recites this Sutra has created a heavier offense than one who slanders the Buddha himself. Slandering the Buddha is a tremendously heavy offense, too, but the Buddha is very compassionate. It doesn't phase him in the least whether you praise him or scold him, and so the offense is less than the offense of slandering the Sutra. Why is slandering the Sutra such a heavy offense? This is because the reciter of the Sutra hasn't yet certified to the unproduced Dharma patience. If he hears you slander him he's likely to get mad and quit reciting. So see what you have done? Not reciting the Sutra, he won't become a Buddha. Sutras are just the Dharma body of the Buddha, and therefore you must not slander them. The Vajra Sutra says, "Wherever this Sutra is, there is the Buddha and his reverent disciples." If this applies to The Vajra Sutra, it certainly applies to The Dharma Flower. The Dharma Flower is the true body of the Buddha. If you want to now see what the Buddha is like, well, then just read The Dharma Flower.

"O MEDICINE KING, YOU SHOULD KNOW THAT ONE WHO READS AND RECITES THE DHARMA FLOWER SUTRA TAKES THE BUDDHA'S ADORNMENTS AS HIS OWN ADORNMENTS." That means that, in

the future, this person will certainly become a Buddha.
"HE SHALL CARRY THE THUS COME ONE ON HIS SHOULDERS." He
is a messenger of the Buddha, teaching living beings,
leading them to proper views. He carries on his back, as
it were, the Thus Come One's Dharma." WHEREVER HE GOES HE
SHOULD BE WELCOMED WITH OBEISANCE, people should bow to
him.

"SINGLEMINDEDLY, AND WITH PALMS JOINED, ONE SHOULD PAY
REVERENCE, MAKE OFFERINGS, HONOR, AND PRAISE HIM.
HE SHOULD RECEIVE THE FINEST OFFERINGS AMONG PEOPLE,
OFFERINGS OF FLOWERS, INCENSE, BEADS, POWDERED INCENSE,
PASTE INCENSE, BURNING INCENSE, SILK CANOPIES, BANNERS,
CLOTHING, FINE FOOD, AND MUSIC, the finest offerings
among people. HEAVENLY JEWELS SHOULD BE SCATTERED OVER
HIM, AND CLUSTERS OF THE FINEST HEAVENLY JEWELS OFFERED
TO HIM.

"WHAT IS THE REASON? Why does he deserve these
offerings? WHEN THIS PERSON JOYFULLY SPEAKS THE DHARMA,
THOSE WHO HEAR IT FOR BUT AN INSTANT SHALL DIRECTLY
ACHIEVE ULTIMATE ANUTTARASAMYAKSAMBODHI." Those who hear
the Sutra can very quickly attain Buddhahood. It won't
take them very long at all.

Sutra: T. 31a 11

At that time, the World Honored One, wishing
to restate these principles, spoke verses, saying:
One wishing to dwell in the Buddha Path

And to accomplish spontaneous wisdom
Should diligently make offerings
To those who receive and uphold The Dharma
*   Flower.*
One wishing quickly to gain
The wisdom of all modes
Should receive and uphold this sutra
And make offerings to those who uphold it.

Outline:

> G2. Verse.
> H1. Exhortation to self-
> practice and benefitting
> others.

Commentary:

AT THAT TIME, THE WORLD HONORED ONE, WISHING TO
RESTATE THESE PRINCIPLES, SPOKE VERSES SAYING: He wanted
to make it easier for living beings to understand the
principles, so he spoke in verses.

Basically, the time is up for this lecture, but I
still have something to say. Someone has some questions
about the different kinds of Dharma Masters and about
inward and outward cultivation.

I told you before, when I was in Kuan-yin Cave in
Hong Kong, my next-door neighbor performed the ceremony
of the flaming mouths every day for a thousand days.
Everyday at about three o'clock he started his ceremony.

He would put on his ceremonial robes and then go out on
the front porch and look up and down the street to see
if any guests were coming. If some guests were coming he
would run in and grab the bells and ring them like mad,
making an unholy racket. When the people walked by they
would see him and think, "This Dharma Master really
works hard," and offer him some money. That's how it
went.

Someone is thinking, "Dharma Master, you always wait
until we all arrive in the evening before you write out
The Shurangama Sutra. Isn't that 'outward' cultivation?"

That's different. I write out the Sutra to teach
you Chinese. Basically, I'm incredibly lazy. I wouldn't
be interested in writing out the Sutra or lecturing,
reading, or reciting it. I like it best when there's
nothing going on at all.

"But you just said that you liked to lecture on the
Sutras!" you say.

That's because the Buddha praises those who lecture
on it. So, I end up liking what I don't like to do!

ONE WISHING TO DWELL IN THE BUDDHA PATH/ Should
there be someone who wants to become a Buddha...If you
want to become a Buddha, you must first dwell in the
Buddha Path. If you don't then you have no way to
become a Buddha.

What is meant by "dwell in the Buddha Path?" It
means that you stand firmly without moving from that

position. It means that you would not change your
persuasions and turn to an outside Way. Originally one
has already taken refuge with the Triple Jewel, and
"dwells in the Buddha Path." But many people stray from
the Buddha Path to study other doctrines. They no longer
dwell in the Buddha Path. Since coming to America, I
have seen many such people. There was one disciple who
had a lot of faith in his teacher. He said, "No matter
what my teacher tells me to to do, I will do it." He
heard that once a disciple had knelt for five hours
asking forgiveness from me, and he said, "I could do that
too. I could kneel for ten hours, and I wouldn't retreat!" I used an expedient to test him out, and
needless to say, he flunked. Not only that, he ran off
to some other religion. He wasn't really dwelling in
the Buddha Path.

Dwelling in the Buddha Path means that you can bear
up under any circumstances. If things are going well,
you can take it. If bad things happen, you can take
that, too. You aren't attached to or turned by favorable
situations. Disliking bad situations means that you are
not dwelling in the Buddha Path. One who dwells in the
Buddha Path cultivates patience. You must be so firm in
your resolve that you can bear up under any adverse cir-
cumstance. Then you can be said to dwell in the Buddha
Path.

AND TO ACCOMPLISH SPONTANEOUS WISDOM/ In order to

dwell in the Buddha Path, you must first have spontaneous wisdom. Spontaneous wisdom is also called "wisdom gained without a teacher." This doesn't mean that it is obtained without a teacher, however. It means that, after the teacher has crossed you over and led you to understanding, then you have spontaneous wisdom and do not rely upon a teacher.

For example as they were about to cross the river, the Fifth Patriarch said to the Sixth Patriarch, "It is fitting that I take you across." The Sixth Patriarch replied, "When one is confused, the teacher takes one across, but when one is enlightened, one takes oneself across."

Before you have crossed the river, you definitely need a boat to cross it, but once you reach the other side, you don't put the boat on your back and carry it around with you everywhere! Your burden would be too heavy; you'd get tired quickly! Once across the river, you must put the boat down. Spontaneous wisdom means that you naturally have wisdom. It is said,

If the demon comes, slay the demon.

If the Buddha comes, slay the Buddha.

How does one obtain spontaneous wisdom? How can one come to dwell in the Buddha Path?

SHOULD DILIGENTLY MAKE OFFERINGS/ TO THOSE WHO RECEIVE AND UPHOLD THE DHARMA FLOWER/ One should constantly make offerings to...who? To the Buddha? No.

Then who, you? No. Me? No. To those who receive and uphold The Dharma Flower Sutra. You should make offerings
to those who can read, recite, receive, uphold, write
out, and lecture upon The Dharma Flower Sutra. Those
who make offerings to such Dharma Masters will be able to
dwell in the Buddha Path and accomplish spontaneous wisdom.

ONE WISHING QUICKLY TO GAIN/ THE WISDOM OF ALL MODES/
Suppose someone else wants to obtain this wisdom very
quickly. The wisdom of all modes is not easy to attain.
Spontaneous wisdom is not the same as the wisdom of all
modes. The wisdom of all modes includes all of existence
in its scope as well as all kinds of wisdom. It is the
perfect wisdom. To realize Buddhahood, one must obtain
the wisdom of all modes. How does one attain it? Don't
be nervous. I will teach you the method.

SHOULD RECEIVE AND UPHOLD THIS SUTRA/If you constantly receive and uphold this Sutra, you will attain
the wisdom of all modes very quickly. Do you see how
wonderful this Sutra is? Why is it titled The Wonderful
Dharma Lotus Flower Sutra? This is where the Wonderful
Dharma is. You need only receive and uphold it to attain
that Wonderful Dharma, the wisdom of all modes. So you
should receive and uphold it and also recite it constantly. You recite it with your mouth and ponder it with
your mind, thinking upon its wonderful principles. With
your body put those principles into action, practicing

them in your daily life. This is called receiving, upholding, and actually practicing The Dharma Flower Sutra.
In this way you can obtain the wisdom of all modes.

AND MAKE OFFERINGS TO THOSE WHO UPHOLD IT/ It's not
enough just to receive and uphold it yourself. You
have to make offerings to others who receive and uphold
it. If you receive offerings from others for your work
with the Sutra, you must pass those offerings on to others
who also work with it. If you can do this you will attain the wisdom of all modes, and you won't be confused
any more. If you obtain spontaneous wisdom, you won't
be stupid any more. Why are you unclear about the principles? Why is it you don't know what's going on? It's
because you haven't attained genuine wisdom. Without
spontaneous wisdom or the wisdom of all modes, your
thoughts will be a mixed bag. One thought will be awakened and the next confused. With one confused thought
you've been bumped off the Buddha Path. With one awakened thought, you are back on it again. If every thought
is awakened, then in every thought you are on the Buddha
Path. If every thought is confused, then in every
thought you are a confused living being. There's nothing
strange about it. It all depends on whether or not you
are confused or awakened.

Who is confused? It's you, yourself. Then who is
awake? It's also just you. Since it's you who wake
yourself up, you should not rely upon anything external

for your awakening.

What is meant by "relying" on something? It's like the poet Li T'ai-po who relied upon wine. Unless he had had a few drinks, he couldn't remember anything at all. He couldn't write poetry or compose essays. But once he had had a few, the muse would visit him, and the poems would flow and the essays spill forth. Hah! Words flowed like a bubbling spring. But first, he had to have the wine. It wouldn't work any other way. He had to have that crutch. Without it, he was helpless. That's "relying."

Some people claim that when they take drugs they can melt into the void. They say drugs give them samadhi. But just take the drugs away and see how far into the void they get. They can't go anywhere then. They are just confusing themselves. Confusing themselves, they are just living beings. Waking themselves up, they are on the Buddha Path. Confusion and awakening are up to you. Nobody can do it for you.

To say nothing of us common folk, even the Buddha's cousin Ananda couldn't rely upon the Buddha for his enlightenment. The Buddha had no way to get enlightened for him. This makes it obvious that you must apply effort yourself. If you just fritter your time away, day after day, that's really pathetic. We say,

An inch of time is an inch of life.

An inch of time is an inch of your life. You must

not waste your time and your life. If you waste all
your time, you will accomplish nothing. If you use it up
entirely, your life will just go down the drain. Everyone should dwell in the Buddha Path everyday. How? Just
don't be confused! If you are confused, you run off the
Path.

"But how can I avoid confusion?" you ask.

Don't ask how you can get out of confusion. Ask
yourself how you got confused in the first place. If
you know how and why it is that you are confused, then
you will know how to get "unconfused."

"I don't know, though," you say.

Since you don't know, I'll tell you. If you knew,
then I wouldn't tell you. Why? Because your self nature
would have taken itself across, and you wouldn't need me
to wake you up. But since you haven't awakened, I'll
teach you a little something...just a little.

You are confused because of ignorance, because of
your not understanding. If you understood, there would
be no problems. If you understood, then the heavens
would be empty and the earth laid bare, and the entire
universe would be yours!

Ignorance is the worst thing going. It's also the
best thing going. Why? Because it's just ignorance that
helps you to become a Buddha. Understanding only comes
from not understanding. Unless there was something you
did not understand, then there would be no way for you

eventually to understand it! Without darkness there is no light. You see? If you can understand precisely this point, you can get enlightened. If you don't understand, you'll just have to approach it gradually--wait a few more days.

Someone says, "I can't wait! I want to understand right now!!"

Okay, already, then understand! You don't have to wait. The understanding is up to you, not me. If you understand you don't have to wait.

Sutra: T. 31a17

One who can receive and uphold
The Wonderful Dharma Flower Sutra
You should know the Buddha sent him,
Out of pity for living beings.
Those who can receive and hold
The Wonderful Dharma Flower Sutra,
Have renounced their pure lands,
And, pitying beings, have been reborn here.
You should know that such people,
Are free to be born wherever they wish,
And can, in this evil world
Vastly teach the supreme Dharma.
One should make offerings of heavenly flowers
Incense and heavenly jeweled garments,

And heaven's finest, most marvelous gems, To the teachers of this Dharma.

Outline:

> H2. Repetition of specific and
> general meanings.
>> I1. Verse of specific explan-
>> ation.
>>> J1. Present.

Commentary:

So hurry up and learn to lecture The Dharma Flower
Sutra! See all the offerings you'll get? But I hope
you won't learn to lecture it out of greed for offerings,
really. You should cultivate and dwell in the Buddha
Path.

ONE WHO CAN RECEIVE AND UPHOLD/ THE WONDERFUL DHARMA
FLOWER SUTRA/ YOU SHOULD KNOW THE BUDDHA SENT HIM. The
Buddha told him to come. If this were not the case, he
wouldn't be able to receive and hold The Dharma Flower
Sutra. If you can receive and uphold The Dharma Flower
Sutra, then the Buddha sent you here. You just don't
know, that's all. It was so long ago, you have forgotten.
You have forgotten your duties. If you read and recite
and uphold the Sutra, then you are the Buddha's messenger.

Why did the Buddha send you here into the evil world
of the five turbidities? OUT OF PITY FOR LIVING BEINGS/

Taking pity on all living beings, the Buddha sent you
into this world. And this evil world of the five turbidities is decidedly impure.

THOSE WHO CAN RECEIVE AND HOLD/ THE WONDERFUL DHARMA
FLOWER SUTRA/ HAVE RENOUNCED THEIR PURE LANDS/ They
themselves wished to renounce their pure lands of reward
and come instead into the evil world of the five turbidities, AND, PITYING BEINGS, HAVE BEEN REBORN HERE/ Because
they have great compassion for living beings, they have
been reborn in this world. YOU SHOULD KNOW THAT SUCH
PEOPLE/ ARE FREE TO BE BORN WHEREVER THEY WISH/ They did not
come into this world on the wheel of rebirth. They pick-
ed this world out of their own choice. They chose to be
born here in order to teach and transform living beings.
AND CAN, IN THIS EVIL WORLD/ In this evil world of the
turbid aeon, the turbidity of views, the turbidity of
affliction, the turbidity of living beings, and the turbidity of the lifespan--such a dirty world VASTLY TEACH
THE SUPREME DHARMA/ They have great fearlessness. They
aren't afraid of the five turbidities, and they aren't
afraid of the ten servants. The ten servants are the
five slow servants and the five sharp servants. Fearless,
they expound upon the supreme Dharma. ONE SHOULD MAKE
OFFERINGS OF HEAVENLY FLOWERS/ INCENSE, AND HEAVENLY
JEWELED GARMENTS/ AND HEAVEN'S FINEST, MOST MARVELOUS GEMS/
The gems are marvelous. In heaven they have jewel-cluster
trays. The tray is empty, but when you put one thing in

it, the whole tray becomes filled with similar things.

For example, if you set a small piece of gold on the tray, the tray will be filled with gold, and so on. Such are the wonderful jewels in the heavens.

TO THE TEACHERS OF THIS DHARMA/ to one who speaks The Dharma Flower Sutra. So I told you to hurry up and learn how to speak the Sutra, but not so that you can get offerings. Offerings shouldn't even enter into the picture. You should learn to speak the Sutra so that you can realize Buddhahood. I don't care if any of you make offerings to me, even though I am speaking the Sutra. If there are no offerings at all, I still keep on lecturing it. I don't do it out of greed for offerings. If I was greedy for fame or offerings, I would be just like Maitreya Bodhisattva! Ahh...

Bodhidharma's disciple, the Bhikshuni Tsung-ch'ih could recite The Dharma Flower Sutra from memory. After she died, a blue lotus flower grew from her mouth as a certification of the merit she had gained through her recitation of the Sutra.

You should arrange in your cultivation for special practices that you undertake, over and above the daily required practices. For example, in addition to morning and evening recitation and translation work and so on, you should concentrate on memorizing or reciting a particular Sutra, The Vajra Sutra, The Dharma Flower Sutra, The Surangama, or The Earth Store Sutra. You should investigate it in great detail and "put it in your stomach!" --i.e., memorize it.

Don't just waste your time all day.

Regardless of whether you have left home or not, you should gather in your thoughts and contemplate emptiness, discipline yourself so that you reduce your bad habits and faults. Change your habits and toss out your faults. Then you will be able to dwell in the Buddha Path and gain a response from the Buddhadharma.

Those who cultivate the Way shouldn't tell people to make offerings of treasures to them. If you take valuable offerings from people, thieves will get interested in you. I say this because there was once an old Taoist named Lu Tung-pin who had the ability to point his finger at a rock and turn it into gold. He turned a lot of rocks to gold for the poor people, but after five hundred years, the gold would turn back into rock. A thief saw this going on and thought, "What an incredible finger that is! If I had his finger I would never be poor again. I could give up this life of crime." He resolved to steal poor Lu Tung-pin's finger. He made elaborate plans to break into his house and cut the man's finger off. Lu Tung-pin may have been an immortal, but he still felt pain when the thief tried to cut off his finger. "Hey, what are you doing cutting off my finger!" he yelled. The thief tried to run away, but Lu Tung-pin who had many assorted spiritual powers, used the power of "Pointing Fixation" and he froze in his tracks. He pointed at him and said, "You can't move." And he couldn't!

Then he asked him, "Why were you trying to cut off my finger?"

"Your finger is just too neat!"

"Huh?"

All you have to do is point to something and it turns to gold. I need your finger, I mean! If I get it, I won't have to be poor."

Lu Tung-pin thought, "This finger might turn things to gold, but it's a lot of trouble too. I'm not going to give it to you, thief and I am not going to use it myself anymore, not commercially anyway."

So cultivators should not have a lot of valuable stuff and you can see why!

Sutra : T. 31a 25

One who can uphold this sutra
After my extinction, in the evil age,
Should be worshipped with palms joined
As if making offerings to the World Honored One.
Fine food and many sweet delicacies
And various kinds of clothing,
Should be offered to this disciple of the Buddha,
Hoping to hear him speak even for a moment.

One who can, in the latter age,
Receive and uphold this sutra,
Has been sent by me into the human realm,
To carry out the Thus Come One's work.

Outline:

J2. Future

Commentary:

ONE WHO CAN UPHOLD THIS SUTRA/ AFTER MY EXTINCTION,
IN THE EVIL AGE/ "My" refers to Shakyamuni Buddha
speaking of himself. The evil age is a time of not only
"five" turbidities, but an uncountable number of turbidities. The evil age is the Dharma-ending age, the age
when people are strong in fighting. Everyone wants to
put everyone else down, to destroy everyone else. People
can't exist side by side. This is a most difficult
age in which to be born and live. So the Buddha thought
of a method. He said, "One who can keep The Dharma
Flower Sutra, SHOULD BE WORSHIPPED WITH PALMS JOINED/
One who can cultivate according to the doctrines in
The Dharma Flower Sutra should be greeted with palms
joined, reverently. You should bow to them just AS IF
MAKING OFFERINGS TO THE WORLD HONORED ONE." The Buddha
gave predictions long ago to those who keep The Dharma
Flower Sutra, saying that they represent him in propagating the Dharma. Therefore, The Dharma Flower Sutra
is extremely important. Why do we say that The Dharma

Flower Sutra is "the Sutra for realizing Buddhahood?"
If you can hear The Dharma Flower Sutra you have a chance
to become a Buddha.

When I was in Hong Kong one of my old disciples,
over 70, always went to my lectures. She couldn't hear
them, however, because she was deaf. Once, when I was
lecturing on the Universal Door Chapter of The Dharma
Flower Sutra suddenly she could hear. She was no longer
deaf. Is this uncanny or not? Once she got her hearing
back, she insisted on attending the lectures even more.
She never missed even one lecture. She would come
regardless of wind or rain. She told people, "If I miss
a lecture, I'm upset for about two weeks, and regret it."

There were also several young students who only
went to my lectures. Even if I told them to go to someone
else's lecture, they wouldn't go! I said, "You can't
just listen to my lectures. The other Dharma Masters
lecture much better than I do. You should go listen to
them."

"Better or not, I'm not going anywhere else," one
of them said. "Why should I go to their lectures? I
could lecture better than they do."

I said, "Don't be so arrogant."

"But there's just no contest!" he insisted "You
can't compare them."

Sometimes I would scold my young students roundly,
but they didn't care. You haven't seen me really get

angry yet. If you had, you wouldn't dare to try to get away with the stuff you do.

As to Sutra lecturers and listeners, it's also a question of inter-personal affinities. If you have affinities with someone, you can scold them, and it won't matter. If you don't have affinities with someone, no matter how much you try to butter them up, they still won't like you. Affinities are very important.

A few days ago I did some nuclear testing. I got angry at my disciples to see if they would run away. Probably, I wasn't tough enough because no one ran away.

FINE FOOD AND MANY SWEET DELICACIES/ Oh boy! Good food. Do you want some? If you do, you can't have any!

This line refers to a great variety of good things to eat, mouth-watering! Who gets 'em? The person who receives and upholds The Dharma Flower Sutra. If you want some, you'd better get to work on the Sutra. But you better get to work on the Sutra anyway, not just to get some good food. That's too greedy! Receive and uphold the Sutra so that in the future you can become a Buddha.

AND VARIOUS KINDS OF CLOTHING/ SHOULD BE OFFERED TO THIS DISCIPLE OF THE BUDDHA/ HOPING TO HEAR HIM SPEAK EVEN FOR A MOMENT/ ONE WHO CAN, IN THE LATTER AGE/ in the future, RECEIVE AND UPHOLD THIS SUTRA/ read, recite, copy it out, or lecture on it, HAS BEEN SENT BY ME INTO THE HUMAN REALM/ Shakyamuni Buddha sent him here TO CARRY OUT THE THUS COME ONE'S WORK/ The Buddha's work is not the work of ordinary people. What is the Buddha's work? Receiving, upholding, reading, reciting, copying out and explaining The Wonderful Dharma Lotus Flower Sutra.

"I am listening to The Dharma Flower Sutra," you ask. "Did the Buddha send me here?"

Ask yourself! Don't ask me. If you have genuine interest in the Sutra and study its principles, then the Buddha sent you here to protect the Bodhimanda. If, in the other hand, you listen, but your mind wanders off to Golden Gate Park, to the beach, or the mountains with their great view, then I believe that you weren't sent by the Buddha, because you aren't really listening to the Sutra, you are false thinking instead. If listening to the lectures makes you very restless, then probably you weren't sent by Shakyamuni Buddha.

Sutra T. 31b2

If for the space of an aeon,
One were to harbor an unwholesome mind
And scowling, scold the Buddha,
He would incur measureless offenses.
But if one were, but for a moment, to speak ill
Of one who reads, recites, or upholds The
  Dharma Flower Sutra,

*His offenses would exceed the former's.
If one who seeks the Buddha Path
Were for the length of an aeon
To stand before me with palms joined,
Praising me with countless verses,
Because of his praise of the Buddha,
He would gain limitless merit and virtue.
But one who praises the keeper of this sutra
Would gain blessings exceeding that.
One who, throughout eighty million aeons
Made offerings to the keeper of this sutra
Of the finest forms, sounds,
Fragrances, tastes, and tangible objects,
And having made such offerings,
Gets to hear it for but an instant,
He should be filled with rejoicing
Thinking, "I have gained great benefit!"*

Outline:

        I2. Verse of general explanation.

Commentary:

IF, FOR THE SPACE OF AN AEON/ ONE WERE TO HARBOR AN UNWHOLESOME MIND/ An aeon is a long time. An unwholesome mind means that AND SCOWLING, SCOLD THE BUDDHA/ Lose one's temper and blow up at the Buddha. Such a person would have to think that they had more personal power than the Buddha. Let's say they kept up their tirade for a whole aeon. HE WOULD INCUR MEASURELESS OFFENSES/ BUT IF ONE WERE, BUT FOR A MOMENT, TO SPEAK ILL/ OF ONE WHO READS, RECITES, OR UPHOLDS/ THE DHARMA FLOWER SUTRA/ HIS OFFENSES WOULD EXCEED THE FORMER'S/ If one were to scold one of the five kinds of Dharma Masters for even a second, to say nothing of an entire aeon, his offenses would be greater than the person mentioned above. So don't speak ill of anyone who lectures on this Sutra, regardless of whether or not they lecture well. For example, I am lecturing on the Sutra now so you shouldn't slander me. Although I am compassionate, I wouldn't be able to lighten your offenses, because this rule was handed down by Shakyamuni Buddha. Nobody can change it.

Notes for the gourmet:

If you don't eat good food, you'll be a little stupider. If you eat a lot of good food, you'll be more stupid. You probably don't believe this, but I sure do. If you don't eat a lot of good food, you can give rise to wisdom. That single thought you had, "I'd like something good to eat," is already stupid! To say nothing of how stupid you get after you stuff yourself, you'll be stupid before you even eat it because if you weren't stupid you wouldn't think, "I want something good to eat." Good or not good, it's just eating. Why have such false thinking about it? Your false thinking is just stupid. Not having that false thought means you are intelligent. You don't have to look for the answers anywhere else. The whole story is told in a single thought. Understand?

I just told you that I can't lecture on the Sutras very well and several people have struck up some false thinking: "The Dharma Master is telling a lie. I know he can lecture yet he is saying he can't."

You're very intelligent. I tell one little lie, and you pick right up on it. Since I can't get away with it, I might as well admit that, yes, I do know how to lecture on the Sutras. Part of the reason for this is because I have set aside my greed for food. I'm not thinking about cookies or anything like that. And before when I said I couldn't lecture, I really wasn't lying. It's really, really the case. If you tried to get me to lecture when I was occupied with eating, I wouldn't be able to do it. The only Sutra I could explain at that time would be the "Gourmet Sutra." So I said not being preoccupied with good food makes one intelligent and thinking about food all the time makes one stupid. No matter whether the food you eat is good or bad, it all turns into the same thing. If you eat some good food, your excrement will stink even more. You might enjoy eating it, but when it hits the toilet you'll think, "Yeccchhh! Whew!" Well who told you to eat that stuff in the first place and get yourself so smelly? A lot

of money will make you all stinky, too. Don't think
that eating too much alone makes you stink. Money will
do it, too. Sometimes we say that high government
officials are "stinky politicians." Well, if Dharma
Masters eat too much good food, they turn into stinky
Masters! I don't want to be one, myself, so I don't like
to eat good food.

All of you disciples should remember this and refrain from developing into stinky Dharma Masters. Okay?

If you're a stinky Dharma Master no one will listen

to you when you lecture on the Sutras. If you speak the
Dharma no one will believe it. You can knock yourself
out trying to tell people how wonderful the Doctrine is,
but people will just stick their fingers in their ears
and refuse to listen. This is like Ch'in-hui who
absolutely refused to recite the Buddha's name. No
matter how they tried to trick him into it, he wouldn't
do it.

So, no one will listen to you. Why? Because you "eat
too well."

IF ONE WHO SEEKS THE BUDDHA PATH/ Who is it? It's
just a person! What are you asking that for! Now, this
person might be you or me. If you seek the Buddha Way,
it's you. If he seeks it, it's him. If I do, it's me.
If you don't seek the Buddha Way, then you're out of the
picture. Anyway suppose this person, WERE FOR THE LENGTH
OF AN AEON/ Not one, two, three years, or a hundred

years...but at least 100,000 years, TO STAND BEFORE ME
WITH PALM'S JOINED/ very respectfully, PRAISING ME WITH
COUNTLESS VERSES, BECAUSE OF HIS PRAISE OF THE BUDDHA/
Although the Buddha doesn't care if people praise him or
not, still you gain more merit by praising the Buddha
than by scolding him. If you scolded the Buddha for an
aeon you would fall into the Avichi Hell. If you praise
the Buddha for an aeon you can reap the fruit of unsurpassed enlightenment. HE WOULD GAIN LIMITLESS MERIT AND
VIRTUE/ Limitless means you couldn't count it. It
wouldn't be as much as the grains of sand in one or two
Ganges Rivers, but as much as the grains in limitless
Ganges Rivers. Would you say that was a lot or not? I
would say it was a lot. You wouldn't dare say it wasn't
a lot. Why? Because you couldn't count it either!
BUT ONE WHO PRAISES THE KEEPER OF THIS SUTRA/ the Dharma
Master who receives, upholds, reads, recites, copies out
or explains The Dharma Flower Sutra, WOULD GAIN BLESS-
INGS EXCEEDING THAT/ This person would have more merit
than the person who praised the Buddha for such a very
long time.

Someone says, "That's just what they say."

Yep, and that's what you just heard. They said it,
and you heard it, and that's the way it is!

The Wonderful Dharma Lotus Flower Sutra is just
that wonderful. You shouldn't ask why the merit gained
by praising the Sutra is greater than the merit gained

by praising the Buddha. Whether you praise the Buddha or
not, he is unmoved. If you praise those who recite the
Sutra, they will be encouraged to be even more vigorous.
If you scold them, and they get mad and quit cultivating
and quit reciting the Sutra, then you have helped to cut
off their Buddha seed. That's a grave offense. I didn't
want to explain this, but several people were wondering
about it, and wishing I would explain it. So, in answer
to the questions in living beings' minds, I am explaining
this mind dharma. ONE WHO, THROUGHOUT EIGHTY MILLION
AEONS/ MADE OFFERINGS TO THE KEEPER OF THIS SUTRA/ OF
THE FINEST FORMS, SOUNDS / the most beautiful things.
FRAGRANCES, TASTES, AND TANGIBLE OBJECTS/--these are the
five desires. Here, they are the best. They are like
those in the Real Reward adornment Land of the Buddha;
they aren't like those in our world. One time Shakyamuni
Buddha was describing the sense objects in the Real Reward Adornment Land, and Mahakashyapa, who had been in
samadhi like an old cultivator, suddenly jumped up dancing. Such an old established cultivator, and he jumped
for joy. It's not surprising that he did, though, con-
sidering how fine things are there. If you want to know
how fine, ask Mahakashyapa. Go ask him: "What's gotten
into you, anyway? Dancing, at your age!!" Then see what
he has to say for himself.

AND HAVING MADE SUCH OFFERINGS/ GETS TO HEAR IT FOR
BUT AN INSTANT/ gets to hear The Dharma Flower Sutra for

just an instant, HE SHOULD BE FILLED WITH REJOICING/

THINKING, "I HAVE GAINED GREAT BENEFIT!"/ I have gained

a chance at Buddhahood. Wouldn't you say that was a

great benefit? What could be better? If you get to hear

The Dharma Flower Sutra, you have a share in becoming a

Buddha. So, the Sutra says,

> "...and say but once, 'Homage to the Buddha,'
>   they shall all realize the Buddha Way."

Sutra : T. 31 b 14

Medicine King, I tell you now,
Of all the sutras I have spoken,
The Dharma Flower is foremost.

Outline:

> H3. Conclusion: praising the Sutra
> as foremost.

Commentary:

Why do I say that The Shurangama Sutra is the Sutra

for developing wisdom and The Dharma Flower is the Sutra

for becoming a Buddha? It's because The Dharma Flower

Sutra is the Buddha's Dharma Body. It's the real body of

the Buddha. It's the Buddha's Reward Body. The Buddha's

clear, pure Dharma Body; Vairochana Buddha is also The

Dharma Flower Sutra. The perfect, full Reward Body,

Nishyanda Buddha is also The Dharma Flower Sutra. The

one hundred thousand million transformation bodies are

also The Dharma Flower Sutra. Within The Dharma Flower
Sutra you will find the three bodies of the Buddha, the
four wisdoms of the Buddha, the five eyes and six penetrations of the Buddha as well. The Dharma Flower Sutra
is the king of Sutras. So now, Shakyamuni Buddha isn't
afraid of taking the trouble to tell Medicine King
Bodhisattva: MEDICINE KING, I TELL YOU NOW/ OF ALL THE
SUTRAS I HAVE SPOKEN/ from the Avatamsaka, through the
Agama, Vaipulya and Prajna periods of my teaching--all
the Sutras I spoke, the final perfect teaching of THE
DHARMA FLOWER IS FOREMOST. The Dharma Flower Sutra is
number one among the number ones! Now, that you are able
to listen to it be explained, even so much as a single
sentence, whether you believe it or not, or understand it
or not, means that you are establishing affinities with
The Dharma Flower Sutra. If you come here to listen to
the lecture, then, in The Dharma Flower assembly you are
setting up affinities. Hearing the Sutra should make you
happier than eating the best of food. If this is the
case, then you have affinities with the Sutra. If you
believe in The Dharma Flower and understand this Wonderful
Dharma, the seed of the wonderful Dharma has been planted
in you. Originally, the wonderful Dharma is something
that cannot be understood, but if now you understand it,
or even if you don't understand it, the seed has been
planted in you. You might want to get rid of it, but you
can't. In the future, when those 2,000 who study become

Buddhas, all with the same name, you will be able to attend their Dharma assemblies. If you are vigorous, then sooner than that you will be able to hear The Dharma Flower Sutra and draw near to all the Buddhas. If you are vigorous, you might become Buddhas before Ananda and Rahula do. Why? Because becoming a Buddha all depends on how vigorous you are. If you are vigorous, you go forward. If not, you fall behind.

Take Maitreya Bodhisattva, for example. He should have become a Buddha long ago. Ananda should have become a Buddha already too, but he concentrated on studying and set himself back behind Shakyamuni Buddha. Maitreya Bodhisattva was seeking fame and so he hasn't become a Buddha yet. Shakyamuni Buddha cultivated vigorously and became a Buddha, and Maitreya Bodhisattva will become a Buddha next. His Dharma Assembly will be called Dragon Flower. So we say,

See you again in the Dragon Flower Assembly! In the future we will all draw near to that fat Bodhisattva, Maitreya. If you want to meet this Bodhisattva, not only can you do so, but you can be him yourself. If your stomach is real big, then you are Maitreya Bodhisattva. If his stomach is real big, then he is Maitreya Bodhisattva. If their stomachs are real big then they are all Maitreya Bodhisattva.

You think, "A big stomach is a lot of trouble. It's

real heavy when you try to walk around and when you eat
you have to eat so much food."

I agree. I had a big stomach for a while, and I
always felt that my two legs couldn't quite support my
body. Now, I have lost weight, and I don't eat too much.
I really hate excess fat!

"Then why does one have to have a big stomach to be
Maitreya Bodhisattva?"

Good question! "Big stomach" means that he is able
to bear up, to be patient and yielding. He bears what
others cannot bear, yields where others cannot yield. He
eats what others can't eat.

This is like when I told my disciple Kuo-hsun, "You
must be able to eat what others cannot eat." This does
not mean that you eat all the good food before other
people get a chance to eat any. It means that you eat
the things other people do not like to eat.

To do what others cannot do means that you do humble
and toilsome work that other people avoid. You do the
dirty work, like cleaning the toilet. Even though we
have very sanitary toilets, they still aren't as fragrant
as the kitchens, right? I am telling it like it is. I
speak Sutras for the common people! If you are a person,
you can understand it. If you are an animal, you might
have trouble! Hah!

So, you bear what others cannot bear. Originally,
if someone above you scolds you or hits you, you might be

able to stand it. But let's say that someone beneath you
scolds you or hits you and you can take it, then that is
genuine patience. You can't say, "I can stand it if my
teacher scolds me, but I can't stand it if my students
scold me." That doesn't count. If my disciples scold me
I bear up. I just think, "They are just my teacher.
There's really no difference." If you can stand being
scolded by your disciples, then you've got some skill.
Or suppose, your own son says to you, "You old man! To
be old and not die is to be a thief!" Hearing this, you
think, "I guess I am a thief. Oh, well, no big deal."
If you can be like that, you've got a stomach pretty much
like Maitreya Bodhisattva's.

To yield where others cannot yield means that you
can give up the things others cannot. Say you have five
million dollars and you give away five hundred thousand,
that doesn't count. If you have five million dollars and
you give away five million dollars, not worrying about
whether you will have any for yourself, that's giving what
others cannot give.

You think, "But that's really stupid!" It's by being
stupid in this way that you can attain great wisdom. If
you don't get that stupid, you can't gain such wisdom.

If you can do these things, it's for sure that you
will accomplish you Way karma. I told these things to
Kuo-hsun, and he left home. He was never greedy for anything. In all the years he spent as my disciple, he

wore the same set of clothes. He never had a quilted
robe or quilted shoes, or anything at all. In Manchuria
it's really cold, and he wasn't afraid of freezing, starving or dying of poverty. He had these "three fearless-
nesses." Later, he immolated himself--he wasn't afraid
of fire, either. His immolation wasn't a political act
of defiance against the government. He didn't do it out
of anger. He felt that the world was filled with too
much pain. He wanted to take the pain of others upon
himself and burn himself as an offering to the Buddha.
He burned himself in front of the Buddha and dedicated
the merit to living beings. So you see that the same
act can have a very different motive and meaning, and
serve a defferent purpose.

Someone like Kuo-hsün did indeed have a "big
stomach." We aren't talking about his regular stomach,
but about his capacity to be patient. It is said,

With his big stomach, he can bear

All the things in the world that are hard to bear.

He opens his mouth to smile,

Laughing at all the funny people in the world.

He just smiles an inconceivable happy smile, mind you,
not a shrill cackle--and laughs at all the people in the
world who are stupidly pursuing fame and profit. He
should be crying, it's so pitiful, but he smiles instead.
They are so upside down he has no way to save them, so he
just laughs instead, and thinks of some way to help

them. Besides, crying makes you stupid and smiling can give you wisdom.

So don't think Maitreya Bodhisattva got his big stomach by overeating. He manifests that appearance as part of his cultivation to teach and transform living beings.

Sutra: T. 31b16

At that time, the Buddha further told the Bodhisattva, Mahasattva Medicine King, "Of all the limitless thousands of myriads of millions of sutras I have spoken, am speaking, or will speak, The Dharma Flower is the hardest to believe and the hardest to understand.

"Medicine King, this sutra is the treasury of the Buddhas' secrets and essentials. It must not be distributed or falsely presented to people. That which the Buddhas, the World Honored Ones, have guarded from the distant past until now, has never been explicitly taught. This sutra incurs much hatred and jealousy even now, when the Thus Come One is present. How much the more so will this be the case after his extinction!"

1588

Outline:

      E2. Praising the Dharma maintained and showing method for propagating the Sutra.

       F1. Prose.

        G1. Praising Sutra-dharma.

        H1. Praising the dharma

Commentary:

AT THAT TIME, having spoken the above verses, Shakyamuni, THE BUDDHA, out of great compassion, fearing living beings might not understand the Buddha's doctrines as set forth in the Sutras, FURTHER TOLD THE BODHISATTVA, MAHASATTVA MEDICINE KING, "OF ALL THE LIMITLESS THOUSANDS OF MYRIADS OF MILLIONS OF SUTRAS I HAVE SPOKEN, AM SPEAKING, OR WILL SPEAK, THE DHARMA FLOWER IS THE HARDEST TO BELIEVE AND THE HARDEST TO UNDERSTAND." The Dharma Flower Sutra is difficult to believe and understand because it is just too wonderful. The wonderful Dharma is wonderful and "unwonderful" people don't believe in it. This Dharma is wonderful and so "unwonderful" people cannot understand it. It takes wonderful people to believe in and understand the wonderful Dharma.

It is also hard to listen to The Dharma Flower Sutra. All of you here are wonderful people. You sit and don't feel uncomfortable or drowsy, and you don't lose interest. Isn't this wonderful?

It is not easy to believe the doctrines presented in this Sutra. For example, above it said that if you scolded the Buddha for an aeon, your offenses, though

great, wouldn't be as great as it you had slandered one
who upholds this Sutra for even an instant. This is not
easy to believe. But if you are a wonderful person you
will believe and understand it. Why can I lecture it to
you? Because I'm a wonderful person. Otherwise, how
could I explain it to you? This is something you couldn't
disbelieve if you wanted to because it's too wonderful!

"MEDICINE KING, THIS SUTRA IS THE TREASURY OF THE OF
BUDDHAS' SECRETS AND ESSENTIALS. Those of you who study
Chinese, why do you learn it so fast? Because by listening to the Sutras it is very easy to develop your wisdom.
Once your wisdom has been opened up, you learn everything
very easily. But don't look upon it as a very simple
process. You don't have any idea how many lifetimes
you have studied in order to have this accomplishment.
This is not a matter of just this one single lifetime,
by any means.

That I can lecture on the Sutras is also not a
matter of one single lifetime. Who knows how many
lifetimes I studied? I remember long ago, I would read
The Dharma Flower Sutra until my eyes bled. Why did
they bleed? Because I didn't sleep for many days. I
just knelt and read the Sutra. The more I read it the
more I wanted to read it and recite it. I forgot about
eating and sleeping. When my eyes started to bleed, I
didn't notice, until the blood fell on the text. Then
I knew, "Oh, those aren't tears, that's blood!" Since

my eyes were acting up like that, I had to rest. That's
how I read The Dharma Flower Sutra.

You say, "Dharma Master, you are really too stupid."

Right. If I was as intelligent as you, my eyes
wouldn't have bled.

Perhaps you are laughing to yourself, "That's right.
That's the way it is."

You may be more intelligent than me, but you are
still my disciples. No matter how smart you are, you're
still studying with me.

I remember in the past, I read a lot of Sutras like
that until my eyes bled. But you shouldn't think that I
was always a Dharma Master. I have done everything. I
was an Emperor, and an official, all kinds of things. I
remember it, more or less. That's why I'm not interested
in being an emperor or a politician, or even a wheel
turning sage king. It's too much trouble. If you can
put things down then there is no trouble.

What is meant by "putting it down?" It means "everything's okay. No problem." You are then a "wonderful
person." The more you listen to the Sutras, the more
wonderful you will find them. If you can't be like that,
then you will have problems listening to the Sutras.
You will sit there thinking "This really isn't very
interesting. It's pretty dry, in fact. It's in Chinese
and has to be translated and uses up a lot of my time.
Wouldn't I be better off out playing somewhere?"

"THIS SUTRA, The Wonderful Dharma Lotus Flower Sutra IS THE STOREHOUSE OF THE SECRETS AND ESSENTIALS OF ALL THE BUDDHAS." It contains the most secret and essential Dharma of the Buddhas in the ten directions. All the Buddhas think it's the most esoteric of Sutras, and they don't speak it explicitly. IT MUST NOT BE DISTRIBUTED casually among people.

"If this is the case," you wonder, "then why have so many copies of it been made to be given to people for study?"

A long time ago, the Buddhas all took this Sutra to be a treasure, and they didn't want to pass it out to everyone. It was a Dharma treasure. This is like the Forty-two Hands, a Dharma which I teach only to my disciples. It's my secret and essential treasury. "OR FALSELY PRESENTED TO PEOPLE." You can't just explain it for everyone. The Buddhas felt this way about The Dharma Flower Sutra. They didn't let everyone see it. They didn't transmit it to people. Wouldn't you say we had a great opportunity now? We get to know all these secrets.

'THAT WHICH THE BUDDHAS, WORLD HONORED ONES, HAVE GUARDED FROM THE DISTANT PAST UNTIL NOW, HAS NEVER BEEN EXPLICITLY TAUGHT. Shakyamuni Buddha says, "The Buddhas of the past took The Dharma Flower Sutra as a secret treasury. Now that I have realized Buddhahood, I have never, until this time, spoken The Dharma Flower Sutra. I spoke the Avatamsaka, Agamas, the Vaipulya, and Prajna

teachings. But THIS SUTRA INCURS MUCH HATRED AND
JEALOUSY EVEN NOW, WHEN THE THUS COME ONE IS PRESENT.
HOW MUCH THE MORE SO WILL THIS BE THE CASE AFTER HIS EX-
TINCTION! Why haven't I spoken The Wonderful Dharma Lotus
Flower Sutra? Do you know? It's because most people
wouldn't believe or understand it. It would have been
useless to explain it. What is more, in speaking the
Sutra, the heavenly demons and those of outside ways
would get jealous." If you try to propagate the proper
Dharma, the demons get angry, because they don't want
people to understand the proper Dharma. If people understand the proper Dharma, then their deviant Dharmas
become useless. Even Shakyamuni Buddha had to be very
careful not to arouse jealousy by speaking the Sutra.
Just before he was about to enter Nirvana, he went ahead
and spoke it anyway, not worrying about it. "If they get
angry or jealous, that's too bad. I'm still going to
speak it. The time has come and I am going to speak it."

Just think how jealous people will get after the
Buddha's extinction. We shouldn't be surprised that now,
as we lecture it week after week, a lot of people get
upset. The demon kings are uncomfortable that we are
propagating the proper Dharma. They feel we are taking
their clientele away from them. Their improper dharmas
no longer are of use so they come here and get angry but
it's no use. The deviant can't overcome the proper, so
they run away.

When Shakyamuni Buddha was in the world, a lot of outside Ways were jealous of the Buddhadharma. Now, in the Dharma-ending Age there are even more outside ways. Some of them claim to have spiritual powers. They say that you can put them in the freezer for a hundred years, and they will come back to life. So what? What use were you during those hundred years? Did you benefit yourself or anyone else? Probably not. And what's more you might not be able to wake up after that hundred years.

There's another outside way where they worship fire. They light their wine on fire and then drink it saying they drink "fire wine." People without much sense see this and think, "I saw it with my own eyes. If they didn't have some kind of spiritual powers, they couldn't do this." But not only do they not have spiritual powers, they don't even have ghostly powers! Obviously the fire won't burn in their stomachs because there's no oxygen it there.

There's another kind of outside way where they say they can walk on fire and not get burnt. It never occurs to people that they could probably do it too--if they walked fast enough! If you want to test them out, ask them to sit down on the fire! If they don't burn then, you could say they had some skill. But even this isn't anything special. It's just deviant magic. These days there are a lot of outside ways. There are some who claim they can drink fantastic amounts of water, even

1594

the whole ocean. What use is that? If they drank up the
entire ocean, all the fish would dry up and die! That
would be terrible. Murder! So, you needn't study these
outside ways.

Sutra: T. 31b21

"Medicine King, you should know that after
my extinction, those who can write out, uphold,
read, recite, make offerings to and explain it for
others, shall be covered with the Thus Come One's
robes and shall also be protected and held in
mind by the Buddhas present in other directions.
These people have great powers of faith, powers
of resolution and vows and the power of good
roots. Know that these people shall dwell together with the Thus Come One and shall
have their heads rubbed by the hand of the
Thus Come One."

Outline:

H2. Praising the people

Commentary:

"MEDICINE KING, YOU SHOULD KNOW THAT AFTER MY
EXTINCTION, THOSE WHO CAN WRITE OUT, UPHOLD, READ,
RECITE, MAKE OFFERINGS TO AND EXPLAIN IT FOR OTHERS..."
Shakyamuni Buddha says that while he is in the world a

lot of people will be jealous of The Dharma Flower Sutra, to say nothing of what it will be like after the Buddha enters Nirvana. Although he says this, still "Medicine King, you should know after the Buddha enters Nirvana, those who can write out, uphold, read, recite, make offerings of incense, flowers, food and drink to, and explain The Dharma Flower Sutra to other people, setting forth its wonderful doctrines, SHALL BE COVERED WITH THE THUS COME ONE'S ROBES." These five kinds of Dharma Masters shall be covered with the Thus Come One's kashaya or sash. This is like when people recite the name of Amitabha Buddha and recite to the point of "reciting and yet not reciting, not reciting and yet reciting." When they attain this state, they can see Amitabha Buddha come and rub the top of their heads and cover them with his sash. This means that in the future they are certain to be reborn in Amitabha Buddha's Land of Ultimate Bliss. Now, if one can receive and uphold The Dharma Flower Sutra, the Thus Come One will cover them with his sash, too. What is more, they "SHALL ALSO BE PROTECTED AND HELD IN MIND BY THE BUDDHAS PRESENT IN OTHER DIRECTIONS." Not only will Shakyamuni Buddha cover you with his sash, but the Buddhas in the ten directions will protect you and keep you in mind at all times, lending you their support and helping you to develop great wisdom.

"THESE PEOPLE HAVE GREAT POWERS OF FAITH." This "greatness" of the power of faith is not that which is

spoken of in relation to "small." It goes beyond the
relative into the realm of the absolute. There is
nothing which compares with the greatness of their
powers of faith. The Buddhadharma is like the great sea.
It can only be entered by means of faith. If you have
no faith, you cannot get into the Buddhadharma. Of
faith it is said,

> Faith is the source of the Way
>
> The mother of merit and virtue.
>
> It nurtures all our good roots.

If you have faith, you will have merit and virtue. If
you have no faith, you will have no merit or virtue.
If you have faith, you will be able to cultivate the
Way. If you have no faith, you will be unable to do so.
Therefore, faith is the most important factor in cultivation. If you can receive, uphold, read, recite, write
out, and explain The Dharma Flower Sutra, that means you
have great powers of faith. If you lack great powers
of faith, you won't be able to do these things. To the
word faith, we add the word "power" and this means that
one has no doubts; one has only faith. "POWERS OF RESOLU-
TION." Once you have faith, you must set up your resolve
and determination. With great determination, you then
make "VOWS." Those vows should be as solid as stone and
as durable as iron. These are the vows you need, vows
to receive and practice The Dharma Flower Sutra.

Faith alone is not

enough if you don't wish to cultivate. "AND THE POWER OF GOOD ROOTS." Why are you able to have faith and determination in your cultivation? It's because of your good roots. The power of good roots refers to the seeds of Bodhi which were planted many lifetimes and many aeons ago. Your good roots then grew day by day. If you had no good roots, you could never encounter The Dharma Flower Sutra.

"You should KNOW THAT THESE PEOPLE who can receive, uphold, read, recite, write out and explain The Dharma Flower Sutra, SHALL DWELL TOGETHER WITH THE THUS COME ONE"--it is just the same as if you were living with the Buddha--"AND SHALL HAVE THEIR HEADS RUBBED BY THE HAND OF THE THUS COME ONE." This is called "getting rubbed on the crown of the head." It is a gesture of the utmost compassion and fondness. The Buddha often rubs the crowns of living being's heads. If he has affinities with someone, he will pat them on the head. In this way the Buddha infuses them with his awesome virtue and eradicates their obstacles. This is referring only to being patted on the head. It doesn't mean that he bestows predictions on them. If he does both, then that living being has a chance to become a Buddha in the future. When you cultivate, sometimes in meditation you might feel that there is something crawling around on top of your head, like maybe a little bug or something. When you have this feeling, what is actually happening is that

the Buddhas of the ten directions have come to pat you
on the head. You should give rise to even more faith and
vows, and truly practice the Buddha Path. Why? Because
the Buddha is being so kind to you and helping you out,
and if you don't give rise to great resolve, you'll be
showing ingratitude towards the Buddha.

Sutra = T. 31b26

"Medicine King, in any place where this
sutra is spoken, read, recited, written out, or
stored, one should build a stupa of the seven
jewels, making it high, broad, and adorned. It
is not necessary to place sharira in it. Why
is this? Within it already is the complete body
of the Thus Come One. To this stupa one should
make offerings of all kinds of flowers, incense,
beads, silk canopies, banners, vocal and instrumental music, honoring and praising it. If
people should see this stupa, bow before it, and
make offerings to it, you should know that
they are close to Anuttarasamyaksambodhi.

Outline:

H3. Praising the place.

Commentary:

"MEDICINE KING, IN ANY PLACE, that is in all places

regardless of where they are, WHERE THIS SUTRA IS SPOKEN, explained, READ, RECITED, WRITTEN OUT OR STORED, wherever the Sutra is, ONE SHOULD BUILD A STUPA OF THE SEVEN JEWELS, MAKING IT HIGH, BROAD AND ADORNED. You shouldn't just make a small stupa. Before, I told you the story of a dwarf, the little man only three feet high but five feet wide. He looked strange, but he had a beautiful voice. Someone asked the Buddha how he could look so strange yet sing so well. The Buddha told him, "In a former life, limitless aeons ago, a man was making a jeweled stupa. This man objected, saying, 'Why are you making it so high? No one will even be able to see the top, for heaven's sake! Make it a little broader and a little shorter so everyone can see it and bow to it!' As a retribution for his discouraging words, life after life he was born as a dwarf. So, if you see short people, you can guess that in a former life, they probably criticised the making of a stupa. The reason for his bell-like voice was because, when the stupa was completed, he hung a bell in the tower." So after this, if someone is building a temple, you shouldn't object to its size saying, "Why don't you make a smaller one? There's not that many people in this area anyway." In general, the higher and bigger temples and stupas are, the better. Stupas are defined as "high, manifest places," or as "square graves." Anyway, since he hung the bell in the stupa, he had a lovely voice. This should illustrate

that if we want a beautiful voice we should hang a bell
in a jeweled pagoda.

"IT IS NOT NECESSARY TO PLACE SHARIRA IN IT." The
jeweled stupa should be studded with lustrous jewels
which shine both day and night. If you have some sharira,
you can put them in, of course, but if you don't, you need
not go all over looking for some to put in. 'WHY IS THIS?
WITHIN IT ALREADY IS THE COMPLETE BODY OF THE THUS COME
ONE. If there is a copy of this Sutra in the stupa, then
the true body of the Buddha is there. TO THIS STUPA ONE
SHOULD MAKE OFFERINGS OF ALL KINDS OF FLOWERS, INCENSE,
BEADS, SILK CANOPIES, BANNERS, VOCAL AND INSTRUMENTAL
MUSIC." To this jeweled stupa, you should make offerings
of flowers, incense, beads, silk canopies, banners, and
instrumental and vocal music. We sing songs and chants
in praise of the Buddha. We really have no way to express
completely our reverence for the Buddha and our sincerity,
so we just use songs which everyone likes to hear to express our appreciation of the Buddha's merit and virtue.
The Dharma is not cultivated to accomplishment by means
of one method only. There are eighty-four thousand
Dharma doors. One can realize Buddhahood by the use of
any one of them'...'HONORING AND PRAISING IT. IF PEOPLE
SHOULD SEE THIS STUPA, BOW BEFORE IT, AND MAKE OFFERINGS
TO IT, or even nod their heads even just slightly or raise
one hand as a gesture of respect, YOU SHOULD KNOW THAT
THEY ARE CLOSE TO, they are not far from ANUTTARASAMYAKSAM-

BODHI, the Buddha fruit." So in the future we should all make a vow, a vow together to make a jeweled stupa for The Dharma Flower Sutra. We should make it as high as possible--higher than the Empire State Building! It should be the tallest stupa in the world. If we make a vow, then we can do it. It depends on how determined we are in our vow. Determination means you set your will to accomplish something, and you don't stop until you do. When I left home I made a determined vow. I said, "In the future I am certainly going to spread Buddhism throughout the entire world. I will bring Buddhism to every place where it is absent now. Not only will I spread the Buddhadharma, but I will spread the true, orthodox Buddhadharma." Now, I haven't fulfilled my vows yet. When there is Buddhism in all worlds, not just this one, then my vows will be fulfilled. It's not enough to have Buddhism throughout just this one world. All of you who make vows and are determined in them will certainly succeed.

The eighth day of the fourth month is the Buddha's birthday (May 10, 1969). It's the most important Buddhist holiday, so we are having a celebration and everyone should do word-of-mouth advertising, that is, tell all your relatives and friends. In the afternoon at 2:00 we are going to perform the Liberation of Life ceremony. Why do we do this? First of all it is illustrative of "non-killing" and the compassion of the Buddha's teaching.

1602

It is said,

>   If in this life you don't cage birds,
>   in the future you won't be put in jail.

In the ceremony, we release birds from their cages so
they can be free to fly. Doing this insures that in
future lives we won't be put in jail. Secondly, if you
liberate creatures, others will liberate you. You may
think, "I'm no bird. I don't need to do this." Maybe
you're not a bird now, but you've forgotten about the
times in the distant past when you were a bird. All of
us, in former lives, have been everything there is to be.
We've all been ants and mosquitoes. On a larger scale,
we've been emperors, generals, everything! However,
greed, hatred, and stupidity have covered up your self-
natures so you can't remember these things.

There are twenty days left until the Buddha's birthday and everyone should get busy and advertise. Don't
wait for the T.V. and radio to do all the work. You
should all be T.V.s and radios. Spread the word!

Sutra : T. 31 c 3

*"Medicine King, many people, both at home
and left home, practice the Bodhisattva Path.
If they are unable to see, hear, recite, write out,
uphold, or make offerings to The Dharma
Flower Sutra, know that these people have not*

yet skillfully practiced the Bodhisattva Path.
If they are able to hear this sutra, then they
will be able to skillfully practice the Bodhisat-
tva Path.

Outline:

H4. Praising the cause.

Commentary:

"MEDICINE KING," Shakyamuni Buddha continues, "MANY

PEOPLE, BOTH AT HOME, that is laymen and laywomen, AND

LEFT HOME, that is, Bhikshus and Bhikshunis, PRACTICE THE

BODHISATTVA PATH. Both laypeople and left-home people

can practice the Bodhisattva Path.

What is the Bodhisattva Path? It means benefitting

other people. It means benefitting oneself and bene-

fitting others. It means being able to put yourself

aside to help others, giving the advantages to other

people and taking the disadvantages upon oneself. The

Bodhisattva Path is like water: Water benefits all things

but never boasts of its merit. All living creatures,

whether they are born from wombs, eggs, moisture, or

transformation, depend upon water for the maintenance of

their life. Without water, they can't live. But water

itself doesn't boast of its merit saying, "I have helped

you so much. My merit is great indeed." Those who

practice the Bodhisattva Path should be this way. Don't

think, "I have helped living beings and so I have merit."

Lao-Tzu said,

> "The highest goodness is like water. Water
> well benefits all things and yet does not contend.
> It goes to places people despise and so it is
> close to the Way..."

Water flows right into lowly places, places where
no one would like to live. When you practice the
Bodhisattva Path, you must give the merit to others and
take the mistakes upon yourself.

"But then I won't have any merit," you object.

The more you give the merit to others, the greater
your merit becomes. On the surface, you are giving the
merit away, but underneath, in the realms of true principle, it remains yours. People who don't understand how
to cultivate are always struggling to grab the spotlight,
to be number one, and to make sure everyone knows who
they are. People who understand true principle don't
seek recognition. It is said,

> "Good done for show, is not truly good.
> Evil done in secret is great evil indeed."

Bodhisattvas don't want people to know about their good
deeds. If they make mistakes, they don't care if people
find out.

The Bodhisattva Path means benefitting yourself and
benefitting others. It means benefitting others more

than yourself, and even benefitting others at your own expense. Bodhisattvas practice the six perfections: giving, holding precepts, patience, vigor, Dhyana samadhi and wisdom. In giving, you should give to other people. Giving doesn't mean to tell other people to give things to you! You can't complain and say, "I am one of the Triple Jewel. How come nobody makes offerings to me?" Holding precepts also means that you hold them yourself. It doesn't mean that you go around telling other people to hold precepts. Patience means you yourself are patient, not that you tell others to be patient. Vigor also means that you are vigorous, not that you tell others to be vigorous and remain lazy yourself. You can't think, "I have already become a Bodhisattva and so I don't need to be vigorous. I'll just tell the new Bodhisattvas to be vigorous. I am an old Bodhisattva, so I don't have to be vigorous."

As to Dhyana samadhi, you must cultivate it yourself. You can't pester people and say, "Hey! Why don't you have any Dhyana samadhi?" Finally, you yourself must have Prajna wisdom. You can't tell others to cultivate it and fail to cultivate it yourself.

The six perfections aren't to be practiced for one day. You must practice them every single day and never rest for even a second. Practicing the Bodhisattva Path means that you are busy working everyday. Busy doing what? Teaching and transforming living beings.

Living beings are drowning in the sea of suffering.
Unless you push yourself a little how are you ever going
to be able to save them all? There is no time for naps!
There is no time for false thinking!! So the text says,
"Many people, both at home and left home, practice the
Bodhisattva Path..."

"IF THEY ARE UNABLE TO SEE, HEAR, READ, RECITE, WRITE
OUT, UPHOLD, OR MAKE OFFERINGS TO THE DHARMA FLOWER SU-
TRA, KNOW THAT THESE PEOPLE HAVE NOT YET SKILLFULLY PRAC-
TICED THE BODHISATTVA PATH. They practice the Bodhisattva Path, but their foundation is not solid, and they
haven't perfected their practice. If there are those who
practice the Bodhisattva Path and ARE ABLE TO HEAR THIS
SUTRA, THEN THEY WILL BE ABLE TO SKILLFULLY PRACTICE THE
BODHISATTVA PATH." We are now able to hear, see, uphold,
read, recite, and write out The Dharma Flower Sutra. The
only thing to be feared is that you won't wish to practice the Bodhisattva Path. If you practice it, you will
certainly perfect it. Once you have done so, the Buddha
Path is then realized as well.

Sutra: T. 31c6
"If living beings who seek the Buddha Path
get to see or hear The Dharma Flower Sutra
and, having done so, receive and uphold it with
faith and understanding, know that these

people have drawn near to Anuttarasamyaksam-bodhi.

Outline:

H5. Praising the fruition.

I1. The proximate fruit.

Commentary:

"IF LIVING BEINGS WHO SEEK THE BUDDHA PATH GET TO
SEE OR HEAR THE DHARMA FLOWER SUTRA AND, HAVING DONE SO,
RECEIVE AND UPHOLD IT WITH FAITH AND UNDERSTANDING...
Having heard the Sutra, they give rise to wisdom. Since
they have wisdom, they then believe in and understand
the wonderful doctrines of The Dharma Flower Sutra.
Since they deeply believe and understand, they then receive it with their minds and uphold it with their
bodies. "YOU SHOULD KNOW THAT THESE PEOPLE, having come
in contact with the Sutra in this way, HAVE DRAWN NEAR TO
ANUTTARASAMYAKSAMBODHI, they are very close to the Buddha-
fruit, the utmost right and perfect enlightenment."

Sutra: T. 31 c 9

"Medicine King, it is like a person who is thirsty and in need of water. Although he digs for it on a high plain, all he sees is dry earth, and he knows the water is still far off. He continues efforts without cease and eventually sees moist earth and then mud. He is then

certain that water must be close at hand.

Outline:

      I2. Setting up the analogy.

Commentary:

  The Buddha now gives us an analogy: "MEDICINE KING, IT IS LIKE A PERSON WHO IS THIRSTY AND IN NEED OF WATER." He's thirsty. His throat is so dry it is smoking. To say nothing of tea, he would be satisfied with just a little water! "ALTHOUGH HE DIGS FOR IT ON A HIGH PLAIN, digs a deep hole looking for water, ALL HE SEES IS DRY EARTH." This refers to people whose ignorance, afflictions, view of self, and arrogance are as high as Mount Sumeru. If you want to dig a well on top of Mount Sumeru, it's very difficult. In the same way, arrogant and self-satisfied people who wish to cultivate, may cultivate and cultivate, but all they will see is "dry earth,"--that is, they will only attain to the stage of "dry wisdom". "Dry wisdom" means that they have a small measure of wisdom, but it's not great, just small. They haven't obtained the water of the Dharma nature; they haven't truly opened up their wisdom. "AND HE KNOWS THE WATER IS FAR OFF." He obtained a small amount of dry wisdom, a state which is somewhat inconceivable. When he sits in meditation, he thinks, "When I meditate I feel my self nature is emitting light! I feel pure in body and in mind, no others, no self. This is not bad at all!" That's dry wisdom when you

think "It's not bad!"   "Not bad" it may be, but
one still hasn't truly opened up one's wisdom. One has
not broken through the black energy barrel--ignorance.
One thinks, "Strange, how could I be in such a wonderful
state? Surely I am to become a Buddha. It's not all a
trick. I have now obtained something I never understood
before." One has seen a bit of "dry earth."

"AND HE KNOWS THAT THE WATER IS STILL FAR OFF. The
true wisdom of the Buddha, the water of the Dharma-
nature's wisdom is still far away. HE CONTINUES HIS
EFFORTS WITHOUT CEASE." This is the most important phrase!
It means he does not stop cultivating. He continues his
work mindfully and never thinks, as the saying goes:

> Sun it for one day.
> Freeze it for ten.

This is like someone who cultivates for one day and then
sleeps for ten. "He continues his efforts without
cease" means that he is vigorous in the six periods of
the day and night. He continues his efforts, day after
day, digging and digging "AND EVENTUALLY he SEES MOIST
EARTH, he obtains a bit of the water of the Dharma nature,
AND THEN MUD, he certifies to the first, second, third,
and fourth fruits of Arhatship. HE IS THEN CERTAIN...
Having certified to the fruit and attained some of the
"flavor," he is assured THAT WATER MUST BE CLOSE AT HAND."
He knows that he will certainly become a Buddha and gain
the water of the Dharma nature.

There is a story about Confucius, the Chinese sage.
Even though he was a sage, in his day he had to undergo
a lot of hardships. When he was teaching in Hsing-t'an,
present-day Shantung, he had over 3,000 disciples. Of
the three thousand, most of them would come and go their
various way, but 100 of them were his close followers
and went with him everywhere. Shakyamuni Buddha had
1250 close followers; Confucius had about one tenth that
many. At any rate, his followers went with him as he
traveled from country to country, and so the hosts would
have 125 or so mouths to feed. At that time, he was
lecturing all across the land, teaching his disciples
of government and he became an official in the country of
Lu. Within three months time he had things so well regu-
lated that it was possible to leave gold laying in the
street, and no one would steal it. He taught all the
people not to be greedy. Also, at night you didn't need
to lock your door. America used to be like this too,
very well governed. No one cared if they locked their
doors or not. Now, that would never do. At the very
least you have to have dead bolts on the doors. In any
case, within three months, the country of Lu was running
very smoothly. But then the country of Ch'i got jealous.
"This is terrible. If this goes on, we're finished!" So
they thought of a plan and made a gift to the King of Lu
of concubines--sort of like present-day movie stars.
They could sing, dance, and do all kinds of things. The

King of Lu spent three days and nights in their company, without showing up at Court for three days. Confucius was so disgusted at the degenerate behavior of the King he left, taking his disciples with him. He talked to other nobles, thinking they would employ him, but no one wanted to listen to him. It's that way today, too. If you try to tell people the truth, they don't want to hear it. If you tell them something false, they are delighted. Because Confucius always told the truth, he became very unpopular. They gave him a lot of respect, but they didn't employ him. He was too "straight." He wouldn't let the rulers get away with anything. He kept on travelling and came to the border of the countries of Ch'en and of Ts'ai and ran out of offerings. No one gave him anything to eat, and he had no money or food. He was unwelcome in both countries. After three days of no food, he was sick from hunger and couldn't even stand up. Confucius said "What are we going to do now?" One of his disciple suggested, "Fan-tan has food!" Fan-tan was a beggar who stored the rice he had begged in a big barrel, like a grain silo. "Let's go borrow some from him."

Who shall we send? All of you are weak from hunger!"

Tzu-lu bravely stepped forward. "I'll go!!" he said "I'm not sick. A little hunger doesn't bother me!"

"Okay," said Confucius, "go ahead." When Tzu-lu reached Fan-tan, he said, "Hey, Fan-tan, my brother, I'm

Tzu-lu, a student of Confucius, and I have come to borrow some rice. Our party is stuck at the borders of Ch'en and Ts'ai with nothing to eat. We know you have rice, and so we would like to borrow some from you."

Fan-tan said, "All right, but only if you can answer my question." Then he spoke a verse expecting Tzu-lu to finish it for him:

> What is more?
> What is less?
> What is happiness?
> What's distress?

Tzu-lu thought a moment and then said,

> Stars are many
> Moons are few
> Marriage makes you happy
> Death makes you blue.

"No!" Fan-tan said, "That's not the right answer." Tzu-lu thought, "I matched it perfectly. What makes you say it's not right?"

"You don't make sense, you crummy beggar." But Fan-tan didn't shell out the rice and Tzu-lu wasn't about to steal it, so he ran back to Confucius and said, "No luck. Fan-tan--that beggar--is totally unreasonable. He gave me a couplet to match. I gave a good answer, but he rejected it. He just didn't want to give us the rice in the first place!"

Confucius said, "What did he say?"

Tzu-lu said, "He asked me, in this world,

What is more?
What is less?
What is happiness?
What's distress?"

Confucius said, "Well, how did you answer him?"

"I said, Stars are many
Moons are few.
Marriage makes you happy
Death makes you blue.

What's wrong with that? It's perfectly all right. It's
great!"

Confucius said, "No, You're wrong."

Tzu-lu didn't dare contradict his teacher.

Confucius said, "You go back to Fan-tan and tell him
this:

Petty men are many;
Sages are few.
If we get the rice we're happy;
If we don't we're blue."

When Tzu-lu said this to Fan-tan, Fan-tan nodded his
head in approval. "You're teacher is much more advanced
than you are. That's fine." And he gave him the rice.
They ate only rice, no vegetables, for several days.
Then a tall black general showed up and ran into the
garden intending to murder them. Tzu-lu had eaten his
fill and was feeling even more courageous than usual. He

started fighting with him. Although he was strong, he couldn't outfight the big general. Confucius was standing in the doorway watching all this and he said, "Yu," using Tzu-lu's other name, "Go for his throat." Tzu-lu got the hint and slit the man's throat. As it turned out, it wasn't a human being, after all, it was a giant fish and it filled up the whole garden. Confucius and his disciples had rice and fish then, and none of them starved to death.

Tzu-lu's strongest point was that he was delighted to hear people criticize him and tell him of his faults.

Sutra: T. 31 c 12

"The Bodhisattvas are also like this. Know that those who have not yet heard, not yet understood, or not yet put into practice The Dharma Flower Sutra, are still far from Anuttarasamyaksambodhi. Those who have heard and understood, thought upon, and put it into practice certainly should be known as coming near to Anuttarasamyaksambodhi.

Outline:

I3. Correlating the analogy to the Dharma.

Commentary:

"THE BODHISATTVAS ARE ALSO LIKE THIS." They are like

those mentioned in the previous analogy. "KNOW THAT THOSE WHO HAVE NOT YET HEARD, NOT YET UNDERSTOOD, OR NOT YET PUT INTO PRACTICE THE inconceivably wonderful Dharma door of THE DHARMA FLOWER SUTRA, ARE STILL FAR FROM ANUTTARASAMYAKSAMBODHI." Although they may practice the Bodhisattva Path, if they have not heard The Dharma Flower Sutra, understood it's doctrines, or cultivated according to them, they are very far away from the Buddha-fruit.

"You should know that THOSE WHO HAVE HEARD, AND UNDERSTOOD, THOUGHT UPON, AND PUT IT INTO PRACTICE..." This represents the three types of wisdom: the wisdom of hearing, the wisdom of thought, and the wisdom of culti-vation. The wisdom of hearing arises when one hears the principles in the Sutras. The wisdom of thinking refers to wisdom arising through contemplating the doctrines and decreasing one's false thinking. If you had no wisdom, if you were stupid, you wouldn't be able to cultivate according to The Dharma Flower Sutra. Not only would you be unable to cultivate, you wouldn't even be able to think about it, and in fact you wouldn't even have a chance to hear The Dharma Flower Sutra. It is through the three types of wisdom, hearing, thinking and cultivating, that one enters samadhi. "...CERTAINLY SHOULD BE KNOWN AS COMING NEAR TO ANUTTARASAMYAKSAMBODHI." Because they understand genuine principle, The Dharma Flower Sutra "opens the provisional and reveals the real."

There is nothing false in it. Therefore, those who understand The Dharma Flower Sutra have great good roots
and great wisdom. If they didn't, they wouldn't have the
opportunity to hear it. You should not think that it's
easy to come and listen to the lectures on the Sutra.
It's extremely difficult. You must make yourself quiet
inside and listen to the Sutra--that's an inconceivable
state. However, your habits from many lifetimes and
many aeons are heavy. You may want to listen to the
Sutra, but sometimes you have false thinking. One person
told me that they felt as if they were two people. One
wanted to listen to the Sutra, the other didn't! A war
was going on between them. Well, the one of you that
wants to listen to the Sutra, that's your original nature.
The one of you that doesn't want to hear the Sutra is
your old habits that make it impossible for you to subdue your mind. You should examine yourself closely and
ask yourself, "Just who is this person who wants to listen to the Sutra, and who is this person who wants to
indulge in false thinking?" When you have figured it
out, you won't listen to those old habits anymore. You
should know that the one who doesn't want you to listen
wants you to fall, to get off the track and fall into
the three evil paths. The one that wants to listen,
wants to keep you on the path and keep you from the three
evil paths. So pay attention! Don't get confused by your
habits.

Sutra : T. 31 c 15

"What is the reason? The Anuttarasamyak-sambodhi of all the Bodhisattvas belongs to this sutra. This sutra opens the expedient Dharma doors. It demonstrates the true, real mark. The storehouse of The Dharma Flower Sutra is deep, solid, recondite, and far reaching. No one could reach it except that now, the Buddha, in teaching and transforming the Bodhisattvas and bringing them to accomplishment, demonstrates it for their sakes.

Outline:

I4. Showing the nearness of
Bodhisattvas to it.

Commentary:

"WHAT IS THE REASON? Why is anuttarasamyaksambodhi near to some and far away from others? THE ANUTTARASAMYAKSAMBODHI OF ALL THE BODHISATTVAS BELONGS TO THIS SUTRA." It is all included within The Dharma Flower Sutra. All the Bodhisattvas are born from The Wonderful Dharma Lotus Flower Sutra. The realization of the supreme Buddha fruit comes from this Sutra as well. The Wonderful Dharma Lotus Flower Sutra is the mother of all the Buddhas and Bodhisattvas of the ten directions.

1618

'THIS SUTRA OPENS THE EXPEDIENT DHARMA DOORS. It
opens up all the expedient Dharma doors--they are not
used anymore. IT DEMONSTRATES THE TRUE, REAL MARK.' It
points to and instructs us in the wonderful doctrine of
the true mark. It points out the principle substance,
that which is complete within all of us. The principle
of the real mark is not obtained from the outside.
Every single person is complete with it.

As to the principle substance of the real mark, on
the part of all the Buddhas, it is not "more." On the
part of living beings it is not "less." It's the same
in all of us. Most people, however, turn their backs
on enlightenment and unite with the dust. Thus they do
not know that they have the real mark. The Buddha shows
us how to turn our backs on the dust and unite with
enlightenment, in this way realizing the true mark.

"THE STOREHOUSE OF THE DHARMA FLOWER SUTRA IS DEEP."
It is deep because the Sutra is complete with limitless
meanings. It is like the great sea, deep and unfathom-
able. "SOLID" means that there are no heavenly demons or
outside ways who could harm the Sutra's wonderful Dharma.
'RECONDITE' means that the doctrines of The Dharma Flower
Sutra are exceedingly abstruse and hard to fathom. They
are secret and hard to see. They "hide out," as it were,
like Heng-yin who cultivates on the stairs where no one
can see her. 'FAR-REACHING,': For living beings to reach
the Buddha-position, they must pass through nine stages--
the nine Dharma realms. Therefore, 'NO ONE COULD REACH

IT," because it is so far away, it's not easy for people
to reach the level of The Dharma Flower Sutra. The
Dharma Flower Sutra tells us that in the future everyone
will realize Buddhahood. This is not easy to believe or
understand. "EXCEPT THAT NOW, THE BUDDHA" opens the
provisional to reveal the real. He does away with
provisional Dharma and points to the real path. IN
TEACHING AND TRANSFORMING THE BODHISATTVAS AND BRINGING
THEM TO ACCOMPLISHMENT, DEMONSTRATES IT FOR THEIR SAKES."
He speaks The Wonderful Dharma Lotus Flower Sutra. So the
Great Master Chih-che read The Dharma Flower Sutra to the
part where Medicine King Bodhisattva burned his body as
an offering to the Buddhas and the text said, "This is
called true vigor. This is a true Dharma offering." As
he read these lines he entered samadhi. In samadhi
he saw the assembly at Vulture Peak still in session.
It had not dispersed. Shakyamuni Buddha was still
lecturing The Dharma Flower Sutra there on Vulture Peak,
and he was listening. Not only was Great Master Chih-
che in the Dharma Flower Assembly, but perhaps you people
were there, too! So now, although you are Americans, you
have this chance to hear The Lotus Sutra in Chinese!!
With translation!! This is in inconceivable state. When
you lecture on The Wonderful Dharma Lotus Flower Sutra,
you're supposed to talk about wonderful dharmas. Well,
my lecturing The Dharma Flower Sutra for you is in

itself a wonderful Dharma. Your listening to it is also
a wonderful Dharma. If it weren't you'd have no way to
hear it.

Sutra: T. 31 a9

"Medicine King, if a Bodhisattva upon hearing The Dharma Flower Sutra is frightened or
afraid, you should know that he is a Bodhisattva of newly resolved mind. If a Sound
Hearer, upon hearing this sutra is frightened
or afraid, you should know that he is one of
overweening arrogance?

Outline:

> I5. Picking out the bad ones.

Commentary:

"MEDICINE KING, IF A BODHISATTVA UPON HEARING THE
DHARMA FLOWER SUTRA IS FRIGHTENED OR AFRAID... He hears
lectures on The Dharma Flower Sutra and thinks "Hey,
how could this be? It's too wonderful. It's impossible.
Is this a demon speaking the Dharma? Is it for real?"
and he gets scared out of his wits. "YOU SHOULD KNOW THAT
HE IS A BODHISATTVA OF NEWLY RESOLVED MIND." He gets
frightened because he is a newly resolved Bodhisattva who
has never heard The Dharma Flower Sutra before. These are
the eighty thousand Bodhisattvas Medicine King brought
along. Bodhisattvas are of the Great Vehicle, but they

get scared if they are just beginners. "IF A SOUND
HEARER, one of the Two Vehicles, UPON HEARING THIS SUTRA
IS FRIGHTENED OR AFRAID, YOU SHOULD KNOW THAT HE IS ONE
OF OVERWEENING ARROGANCE." He thinks, "What's this all
about?" Those of overweening arrogance don't believe in
anything. They don't believe in their teacher, in the
Buddha, the Dharma, or the Sangha. You can lecture and
teach with great energy, but they let it all pass in one
ear and out the other. Overweening arrogance was the
fault of the five thousand people who walked out in the
beginning of The Lotus Sutra. The Buddha said, "It's
good that those of overweening pride have left. Now,
only the best people remain, the most sincere."
The text here refers to these five thousand, and also to
those in the future who run off when they hear that the
Sutra is going to be lectured. They don't respect their
teachers, the Buddha, the Dharma, or the Sangha. All day
long, they just don't know what they are doing--they are
those of overweening arrogance.

Sutra: T. 31c 21

Medicine King, if there is a good man or a good woman, after the extinction of the Thus Come One, who wishes to speak The Dharma Flower Sutra for the sake of the four assemblies, how should they speak it? This good man or good woman should enter the Thus Come

One's room, put on the Thus Come One's robe, sit on the Thus Come One's throne, and only then expound upon this sutra for the sake of the four assemblies.

Outline:

> G2. Demonstrating the model.
> H1. The model itself.
> I1. The statement.

Commentary:

"MEDICINE KING, IF THERE IS A GOOD MAN OR A GOOD WOMAN" -- perhaps they have left home, or perhaps they are at home "AFTER THE EXTINCTION OF THE THUS COME ONE," after the Buddha has entered Nirvana "WHO WISHES TO SPEAK THE DHARMA FLOWER SUTRA FOR THE SAKE OF THE FOUR ASSEMBLIES, Bhikshus, Bhikshunis, Upasakas, Upasikas, HOW SHOULD THEY SPEAK IT? How should they go about lecturing upon it? I will tell you. THIS GOOD MAN OR GOOD WOMAN SHOULD ENTER THE THUS COME ONE'S ROOM, PUT ON THE THUS COME ONE'S ROBE, SIT ON THE THUS COME ONE'S THRONE, AND ONLY THEN when these conditions have been met, can they EXPOUND UPON THIS SUTRA FOR THE SAKE OF THE FOUR ASSEMBLIES."

Tomorrow we will discuss what is meant by entering the Thus Come One's room, putting on the Thus Come One's robe, and sitting upon the Thus Come One's throne.

Sutra : T. 31c 25

"The Thus Come One's room is the mind of

great compassion towards all living beings. The Thus Come One's robes are the mind of gentleness and patience. The Thus Come One's throne is the emptiness of all Dharmas.

Outline:

I2. The explanation.

Commentary:

If after the Thus Come One's extinction, you wish to speak The Dharma Flower Sutra for the sake of the Bhikshus, Bhikshunis, Upasakas and Upasikas, you must enter the Thus Come One's room, put on the Thus Come One's robes, and sit on the Thus Come One's throne. After that, then you can lecture upon The Dharma Flower Sutra.

What is meant by "the Thus Come One's room?" Does it actually mean the room where he lives? There are a great many people who lecture on the Sutras, but the Thus Come One has only one room. Obviously, they all won't fit. Even though he has spiritual powers with which he can take the limitless into one and expand the one into the limitless, still that's just a temporary arrangement. After awhile it's bound to get crowded. Do we move the Thus Come One's room to the place where you are and give it to you alone to live in? Then where would the Thus Come One move to?

"Doesn't he have a lot of rooms? Couldn't he go somewhere else?"

If he did, then the room he vacates would no longer be "his" room! Besides, all the Dharma Masters are in different countries; they can't all move to one place to live in the Thus Come One's room. So ultimately, what do we mean by "the Thus Come One's room?" All living beings are complete with the "Thus Come One's room." They don't all have to move house. Nobody has to re-locate at all.

The text says, "THE THUS COME ONE'S ROOM IS THE MIND OF GREAT COMPASSION TOWARDS ALL LIVING BEINGS." If you have a heart of great compassion, just that is the Thus Come One's room. With a heart of great compassion, you pity all living beings. If living beings slander you, you don't get angry. If they scold you, you get angry even less. You maintain an attitude of loving kindness towards those who have no affinity with you and an atti-tude of great compassion towards those with whom you feel at one. "Having no affinity" means that a person is not well disposed towards you. The more they don't like you, the kinder you should be to them. Kindness means making people happy. To feel at one with living beings means that when living beings suffer, you look upon it as your own suffering, and you find a way to relieve them of their suffering. Kuan Shih Yin Bodhisattva has great compassion. She sees the sufferings of living beings as her own sufferings and rescues people from suffering. If you can have great kindness towards those with whom you lack affinities and great compassion towards those of one substance, then you have entered the Thus Come One's room.

"THE THUS COME ONE'S ROBES ARE THE MIND OF GENTLENESS AND PATIENCE." This means that you have no "fire" at all. Even if one's disciples bully you, or your children bully you, you don't get angry. One is very compliant and gentle, harmonious and patient. It is not easy to be patient, especially for young people. Patience doesn't mean that if the police come and beat me up, I bear it. It means, let's say you are the policeman and the criminal beats you, you don't get angry. It means that when those beneath you treat you unkindly, you can be patient. When your superiors appear upset with you and you can bear it, that doesn't count as true patience. Let's say your teacher gets mad at you and you don't get mad back; that's not counted as patience. Basically, you're expected not to get angry. But when your peers try to boss you around or get mad at you and you aren't moved, that counts as patience.

"All right, then," you think, "I'm going to get mad at one of my friends and see if he can be patient. In this way I'll be helping him to accomplish his karma of the Way."

"Great. You help him accomplish his karma of the

Way, but who is going to help you do it? When you get tested, will you be patient? If you can be patient yourself, then you can test others, but if you can't, you've got no business testing other people. You must perfect yourself first. The robes of the Thus Come One, then, represent patience and gentleness, not blazing ignorance.

'THE THUS COME ONE'S THRONE IS THE EMPTINESS OF ALL DHARMAS ." All Dharmas are empty.

"Empty?" you say. "Does that mean I'm just supposed to forget everything?"

Emptiness doesn't mean just getting rid of everything. It means to see the emptiness within existence. When it's time to use them, dharmas are there. Otherwise, they are empty. This is like when you cultivate patience, you do it in situations that require patience. Cultivating patience doesn't mean that you are obsessed with the concept of patience at all times, reciting "Patience, patience, patience," all day long, and then when something happens that goes against the grain you still get mad, get upset. Say you can't stand it when people get angry at you, and everyday someone comes up and scolds you. You can't use your patience dharma then. When nothing is happening in that area, you don't need to be preoccupied with patience. You must study all dharmas, but realize their emptiness at the same time. If you don't understand that they are empty, you will form an attachment

to dharmas. Those who study the Dharma must see people
and dharmas as empty. If people aren't seen as empty,
you will be attached to people. If dharmas aren't seen
as empty, you will form an attachment to dharmas.
Therefore, you must sit on the Thus Come One's throne
to lecture The Dharma Flower Sutra. This means that
dharmas must also be made empty. That's the Thus Come
One's throne.

Sutra : T. 31 c 27
"Established securely in these one may then,
with an unflagging mind expound upon The
Dharma Flower Sutra for the sake of the Bodhisattvas and the four assemblies.

Outline:

I3. Exhortation to cultivation.

Commentary:

"ESTABLISHED SECURELY IN THESE," in the mind of great
compassion, the mind of gentleness and patience, and in
the emptiness of all Dharmas,"ONE MAY THEN WITH AN
UNFLAGGING MIND..." I tell you all the time, "Don't be
lazy, Don't be lazy." That's just what The Dharma Flower
Sutra tells you,too. If you want to lecture on the
Dharma Flower Sutra you must not be lazy. A flagging
mind is the opposite of a vigorous mind. With a vigorous

mind you may then"EXPOUND UPON THE DHARMA FLOWER SUTRA FOR THE SAKE OF THE BODHISATTVAS AND THE FOUR ASSEMBLIES." The Dharma Flower Sutra is a Dharma for teaching Bodhisattvas; it is a Dharma of which the Buddhas are mindful and protective. If you lecture on the Dharma Flower Sutra, all the Bodhisattvas, the Bhikshus, and Bhikshunis come to listen. In listening to the Sutra, you shouldn't think it's such a simple matter. You have to be at the Bodhisattva level before you can hear The Dharma Flower Sutra. You must be at the level of the Bhikshus, Bhikshunis, Upasakas, and Upasikas before you can hear the Dharma Flower Sutra.

In speaking the Dharma, why do we say it is the "Wonderful" Dharma Lotus Flower Sutra? When you lecture on the Sutra, all the gods, dragons, and the eightfold division of ghosts and spirits all come to listen. The Dharma rain nourishes all the living beings and so it is said to be "wonderful."

Sutra: T. 31 c 28

" Medicine King, from another country, I will send transformed people to gather an assembly of Dharma listeners. I will also send transformed Bhikshus, Bhikshunis, Upasakas, and Upasikas to listen to the Dharma being spoken. All these transformed people, *hearing the Dharma, will believe it and accept it, and comply with it without objection. If one speaks the Dharma in an uninhabited place, I will send gods, ghosts, spirits, gandharvas, asuras, and so forth, to listen to him speak the Dharma. Although I am in another country, I will at all times cause the speaker of Dharma to be able to see me. Should he forget a single punctuation mark of the sutra, I will remind him of it, causing his knowledge to be perfected."*

Outline:

H2.   The five benefits.

Commentary:

This section tells of five benefits accruing to the speaker of The Dharma Flower Sutra.

Shakyamuni Buddha calls out, "MEDICINE KING, FROM ANOTHER COUNTRY, after I have entered Nirvana from this Saha world, I will go to another country to teach and transform living beings. Although I will be in another country, if there are people who enter the Thus Come One's room, put on the Thus Come One's robes, and sit on the Thus Come One's throne, that is, if there is such a Dharma Master who speaks upon The Dharma Flower Sutra I WILL SEND TRANSFORMED   PEOPLE TO GATHER AN ASSEMBLY OF

DHARMA LISTENERS." This is the first benefit, that of the Buddha's sending transformation people. "Transformed" means they are created by transformation. There are two ways to explain it. First, perhaps the Buddha will appoint gods to transform themselves into people. Or perhaps right when the lecture is going on, the people will show up in the audience, and nobody knows where they came from or where they went. Nobody recognizes them at all. Perhaps, they are transformed people sent by Shakyamuni Buddha, but no one recognizes them. Or else you could say that the transformed people look like friends of yours. You see them and think, "Oh, my friend has come to the lecture!" Then when the lecture is over you ask your friend, "Say didn't I see you at the lecture last week?"

And he says, "No! I didn't go."

"But I saw you there!" That's a transformation person. Some transformed people are born into the world just for the purpose of attending your Dharma lectures when the time comes. Others appear on a temporary basis now and then. They don't come from anywhere or go any- where. Now do you understand? You are all transformed people! That's why you are here listening to the Sutra now.

"I don't believe it," you say.

You don't believe it now, but when the time comes for you to believe it, you'll believe it. You just don't believe it right now. In the future you will. So much for transformed people.

"TO GATHER AN ASSEMBLY OF DHARMA LISTENERS." What will the transformed people do? They will round up people to listen to the lectures. They will tell their friends and relatives to come and listen to the Dharma. This is like Kuo-yu whose father just called. You should tell your father to come to the lecture--because you're a transformed person! That's your job. You should know that by bringing people to the lectures you create a great deal of merit for yourself. If they come to the lecture and hear a sentence which causes them to gain enlightenment, then you will have a share in helping them gain enlightenment. By helping others to become Buddhas, you yourself will become a Buddha--it's unavoidable, in fact. So if you have relatives and friends, brothers and sisters, you should encourage them to come to lectures. It's very important. You can't just be an independent Arhat. You can't think, "I'm just going to take care of myself. Why should I worry about them?"

"I WILL ALSO SEND TRANSFORMED BHIKSHUS, BHIKSHUNIS, UPASAKAS, AND UPASIKAS TO LISTEN TO THE DHARMA BEING SPOKEN." So all of you have been transformed to come here and listen to the Dharma. "ALL THESE TRANSFORMED PEOPLE, HEARING THE DHARMA, WILL BELIEVE IT AND ACCEPT IT, AND COMPLY WITH IT WITHOUT OBJECTION." This is the second benefit, that of the Buddha's sending transformations of the four assemblies. They will not object to the way you lecture on the Sutra. They won't say, "You lectured it wrong!! That's not the way to explain it!!" They will be satisfied with whatever explanation you give.

"IF ONE SPEAKS THE DHARMA IN AN UNINHABITED PLACE where no one else is, I WILL SEND GODS, DRAGONS, GHOSTS, SPIRITS, GANDHARVAS, musical spirits in the heavens, and ASURAS who like to fight, AND SO FORTH, TO LISTEN TO HIM SPEAK THE DHARMA." This is the third benefit, that of the Buddha's sending transformations of the eight-fold division.

'ALTHOUGH I AM IN ANOTHER COUNTRY, I WILL AT ALL TIMES CAUSE THE SPEAKER OF DHARMA TO BE ABLE TO SEE ME." This is the fourth benefit, that of seeing the Buddha. Does this mean the Dharma Body, the Reward Body, and the Transformation Body of the Buddha? Yes. What is the Dharma Body. It's The Dharma Flower Sutra. What is the Reward Body? It's The Dharma Flower Sutra. What is the Transformation Body? It's also The Dharma Flower Sutra. If you get to see The Dharma Flower Sutra, you are seeing the true body of the Thus Come One. In hearing The Dharma Flower Sutra you are hearing the true body of the Buddha. Therefore, you shouldn't look for the Thus Come One outside of The Dharma Flower Sutra. The Dharma Flower Sutra itself is the Thus Come One's true body.

"SHOULD HE FORGET A SINGLE PUNCTUATION MARK OF THE SUTRA, I WILL REMIND HIM OF IT, CAUSING HIS KNOWLEDGE TO BE PERFECTED." This is the fifth benefit, that of gaining "Dharani." If he forgets some part of the Sutra when he

is lecturing, I will remind him so that he will remember
it all. You shouldn't get attached and think that the
Buddha is actually going to whisper it in your ear. The
Buddha will help you to remember it for yourself. He will
give you some wisdom so that you can remember what you
have forgotten.

"I don't quite believe this," you say. "Before I
believed in the Buddha, sometimes in school I would
forget things and then suddenly think of them."

"Well, who reminded you of those things? It was
also the Buddha because you have the Buddha's wisdom
and virtuous characteristics, and there is a connection
between you and the Buddha. Therefore, whether you
believe in the Buddha or not, that wisdom is all through
the help of the Thus Come One.

As I said, you are all transformed people. If you
admit it, you are. If you don't, you are, too. Those
who listen to The Dharma Flower Sutra are all transformed
people. That's for sure. The Buddha told us this long
ago, and we shouldn't deny it. Not only should we be
transformed people, we should be transformed Buddhas.
On the 10th of May we are going to bathe the transformed
Buddha on the Buddha's birthday. In the past the
Buddha's birthday was held by various Buddhist groups,
but this year there are real Bhikshus and Bhikshunis, so
the Buddhist Lecture Hall will conduct it. I won't be in
charge, but my young disciples we be. I told you long

ago that I appointed Kuo-ning as Chairperson and Kuo-
ch'ien as the advisor. All of you transformed people
will go there to participate in the Dharma Assembly.
Those of you who can lecture, should give talks. You
can't act like you're dumb.
Those who don't lecture should go and support the
Bodhimanda. In the future you will lecture. This year
we are going to do the Incense Praise and the Eighty-eight
Buddha Repentance. This is the first time this has been
done in America. Next year we will do it again.

Sutra : T. 32 a 6

*At that time, the World Honored One, wishing
to restate this meaning, spoke verses saying,*
   One who wishes to get rid of laxness,
   Should listen to this sutra.
   This sutra is hard to hear,
   And those who believe it and accept it are also
      rare.

Outline:

F2. Verse.
G1. General exhortation.

Commentary:

AT THAT TIME, THE WORLD HONORED ONE wanted to make
things even clearer, WISHING TO RESTATE THIS MEANING,
SPOKE VERSES, SAYING, these verses arose from his great
compassion.

ONE WHO WISHES TO GET RID OF LAXNESS/ laxness means laziness. Why are people lazy? Because they like to take it easy. They don't like to move their arms and legs! Their hands don't like to work, and their legs don't like to walk. They prefer to sit or lie down and rest. As a rule, people don't like to quit being lazy. The Dharma Flower Sutra here is talking about someone who does want to give up their habit of being lazy. To get rid of laziness, you need a method, a plan. SHOULD LISTEN TO THIS SUTRA/ If you want to get rid of it, here's the plan. It's not difficult at all. Just listen to The Dharma Flower Sutra. In this way you can get rid of your laziness. The Dharma Flower Sutra teaches you to be vigorous. When you hear it, you can change. THIS SUTRA IS HARD TO HEAR/ Not just everyone gets a chance to hear The Dharma Flower Sutra. It's very, very hard to come by, and very hard to hear. AND THOSE WHO BELIEVE AND ACCEPT IT ARE ALSO RARE/ Should you get chance to hear it, it's then hard to believe it. If you don't believe it, there is no way you can put it to use and gain its advantages.

Sutra : T. 32 a 10

It is like a person thirsty and in need of water
Who digs for it on a high plain,
And sees only dry, parched earth,
And knows that water is still far off.

Gradually he sees moist earth and then mud,
And knows for sure that water is near.

Outline:

> G2. Verses concerning prose text.
> H1. Verse about fruition.
> I1. Setting up the parable.

Commentary:

IT IS LIKE A PERSON THIRSTY AND IN NEED OF WATER/
This represents common people who are seeking the "water"
of the Buddha fruit. On the ground of the common person
it is very dry, and so one wishes to drink the Dharma
water and realize the Buddha fruit. WHO DIGS FOR IT ON
A HIGH PLAIN/ digging a well. This represents cultivating the Way. Your cultivation is like digging a well.
AND SEES ONLY,DRY, PARCHED EARTH/ This means that because
your arrogance and pride are as high as Mount Sumeru,
you cultivate coming and going but are always on dry
ground. You haven't reached moist ground. You are on
the ground of dry wisdom. You cultivate, attain a
principle, but you are still far from water. AND KNOWS
THAT WATER IS STILL FAR OFF/ You are still far from
Buddhahood, yet you know that eventually you will gain
it. GRADUALLY HE SEES MOIST EARTH AND THEN MUD/ After
you gain dry wisdom you keep digging and gradually you
see "moist earth", that is, you gain a bit of the flavor
and advantage of cultivation. "And mud", means you
attain the first, second, third, or fourth fruits of

Arhatship. AND KNOWS FOR SURE THAT WATER IS NEAR/ You

are sure that in the future you will realize Buddhahood.

To explain the analogy in terms of the five periods

of the Buddha's teaching, the high plain also represents

the Avatamsaka Period. If we want to understand The

Avatamsaka Sutra, it's like being on a high plain

and digging a well. You dig and dig, but you just

can't understand the Avatamsaka's principles. Then, you

go to the Agama Period which is like the dry earth and

investigate it. Then you go to the Vaipulya Period.

This is like seeing moist earth. The Prajna Period is

like seeing mud. The Prajna teaching is the pivotal

point of the teachings where the wealth is passed on from

the Vaipulya Period, through the Prajna Period, into the

Lotus-Nirvana Assembly. In the Prajna teaching the

Buddha's "will" is made out. The Lotus-Nirvana Period

is the Buddha's complete body. It is like finding water.

When one begins to cultivate it is very difficult.

One feels that one cultivates and cultivates but doesn't

get anything. One learns so much Dharma, and it's still

as if there's nothing at all. There's nothing you can

grab onto. You can't see it. You can't hear it. You

can't even think about it! It's very, very difficult.

But you still must continue working without cease. You

continue working and you still don't get anything! It's

like dry, parched earth. Then, after a time, things

start to get interesting. One sees moist earth. One

goes forward and feels that one has developed some
wisdom and obtained the "mud" of Prajna, finally, one
certifies to the water of the Dharma Flower, to the
doctrines of The Dharma Flower Sutra. These doctrines
are endless. They have no beginning, no end, no inside,
no outside. They are not great or small. They are in-
effably wonderful, wonderful beyond words. The Dharma
Flower is truly wonderful Dharma. Only the word "wonderful" can approximate the doctrines of The Dharma Flower.
One who drinks the water of The Dharma Flower will never
be a ghost again. What will one become? One will become
a Buddha. Why would one become a ghost? Because one
never drank The Dharma Flower water. Why would one
become an animal? Because one never got the mud of Prajna.
These birds, you see, never got the mud of Prajna--thus,
their bird-existence. You can explain it this way.

There are many ways to explain the doctrines, because they are endless, wonderful Dharmas. We shall now
explain the analogy according to the Four Additional
Practices: Heat, Summit, Patience, and Highest Mundane
Dharmas. Let us say that a person cultivates the Way.
He is "searching for water." He first comes to the
position of "heat". He doesn't know where it comes from,
but it's warm. Eventually, he reaches the position of
the "summit," the highest point. He is "digging on a
high plain". Like a newborn child who doesn't understand
anything, he is at the position of summit and cannot go

forward. He just has to sit tight. This is called "patience". You can't strike up false thinking and run off, or else you might get caught by demons or ghosts. So you "continue your efforts without interruption." At the summit, you have to just stay there and be patient. You can try like Monkey to do a somersault across 108,000 miles, but you might not make it back. So even if you want to run, you can't. You have to remain at the position of patience. Having cultivated at the position of patience, you gain the moist earth and the mud. Then, at the position of "highest of worldly Dharmas," you get to drink the Dharma Flower water.

You see, there are countless ways to explain the Dharma. You could never finish explaining all the doctrines. If you know how to listen to the Sutras, even if I didn't explain the principles, you would understand them. If you don't know how to listen, even if I do explain the principles, you still won't understand them.

"What is he talking about? Water? Mud? Dry earth? Warmth? Summit? What is all this?" you would wonder.

You don't know? Well I don't either!

****

This afternoon we are going to "liberate life." Americans see this as strange and wonder why it is done. We do it so that living beings can be free, so they don't

have to be kept in cages. We also do it to nurture our
compassionate hearts by giving creatures their freedom.
By not killing we are cultivating compassion. In letting
living creatures go we also cultivate compassion. Our
compassionate hearts grow larger everyday until they are
as large as the heart of the greatly compassionate
Bodhisattva Kuan Shih Yin. Kuan Yin Bodhisattva did not
kill living beings. She always liberated beings, and so
she has a great compassionate heart. We should imitate
the great kindness and great compassion of Kuan Yin
Bodhisattva and liberate life. It's all very logical.
If you liberate life it increases your compassion.
Liberating life is just liberating yourself. Why? Because you and all living beings are basically one
substance. Living beings and oneself are the same. If
someone put me in a cage, wouldn't I be uncomfortable?
Wouldn't I wish that someone would let me go? If I were
put in jail I wouldn't want to live there. Likewise, I
don't like to see birds put in cages. This is because
living beings and myself are of one substance. Since I
feel this, I want to liberate life.

What is more, you don't know which living being was
related to you in a former life. One might have been
your father, your brother, or your sister. You can't
know for sure. Perhaps they were your children or your
friends. Right now you haven't gained the heavenly eye
or the penetration of past lives so you don't know the

cause and effect. When you see these creatures, you feel uncomfortable and want to set them free. Setting them free isn't stupid by any means, as some people might think. It is a part of cultivation. There isn't just one road in cultivation. There are eighty-four thousand Dharma-doors in cultivation, and every single door leads to the realization of supreme enlightenment. Liberating life is one of them.

In America, in the past, very few people understood this. We are leading the way in this regard and instituting the custom so that people can understand this Dharma. Be careful not to call it "stupid." If you think that way, you will obstruct your own cultivation.

I just said that we wouldn't want to be locked in jail. I will tell you a true dharma. This not an analogy. Your own body is, in fact, a cage! You are stuck in your own body, and you can never get out of it. I just discussed the four positions--warmth, summits, patience, and highest of worldly dharmas. You have never reached the summit, patience, or the highest of worldly dharmas. When you make it to the highest of worldly dharmas, then you will have escaped from the cage of your body. You will have "liberated" your own "life." That's the real liberation of life. This is some real principle I'm telling you here. If you want to liberate your own life you must first liberate these little creatures' lives. One kind of liberation helps the other kind of liberation of life. Liberating life is a very important part of Buddhist practice. But if you haven't understood it, you might think it very ordinary. If you don't cultivate one kind of liberating life, you can't obtain the other kind. There are many changes and transformations. Don't look upon it lightly. The liberating of life brings great returns on your efforts. Don't criticize Dharma-doors that you can't understand. Perhaps now you understand, perhaps you don't.

Sutra : T. 32 a 13

> Medicine King, you should know
> In this way, those people
> Who do not hear The Dharma Flower Sutra
> Are very far from the Buddha's wisdom.
> Those who hear this profound sutra,
> Will thoroughly understand the Sound Hearer
>   Dharmas.
> This is the king of sutras
> And as to those who hear it and ponder upon it,
> you should know that such people,
> Have drawn close to the Buddha's wisdom.

Outline:

I2. Correlating to the Dharma.

Commentary:

Shakyamuni Buddha call out again, MEDICINE KING,

YOU SHOULD KNOW/ IN THIS WAY, THOSE PEOPLE/ the ones I just talked about WHO DO NOT HEAR THE DHARMA FLOWER SUTRA/ARE VERY FAR FROM THE BUDDHA'S WISDOM / You should know that after my extinction, all those people, gods, dragons, or spirits of the eightfold division who do not hear this Sutra will not have an opportunity to become Buddhas. Why not: Because they don't have the Buddha's wisdom. It will be a long time before they become Buddhas. THOSE WHO HEAR THIS PROFOUND SUTRA/ The Wonderful Dharma Lotus Flower Sutra, this profound, far reaching, and wonderful Dharma, WILL THOROUGHLY UNDERSTAND THE SOUND HEARER DHARMAS/ They will understand that the Sound Hearer Dharmas are not ultimate. They will have genuine understanding of this fact. They will know that those of the Two Vehicles haven't reached the ultimate point, but must still go forward. They must cultivate the Bodhisattva Path, the six perfections and the ten thousand conducts, for these are the Dharmas for realizing the Buddha Path.

THIS IS THE KING OF SUTRAS/ AND AS TO THOSE WHO HEAR IT AND PONDER UPON IT/ YOU SHOULD KNOW THAT SUCH PEOPLE/ HAVE DRAWN CLOSE TO THE BUDDHA'S WISDOM. Those who hear this Sutra and who then very carefully ponder upon its meaning...This doesn't mean false thinking. It means thinking it over, meditating on it, like when you think on the topic, "Who is reciting the Buddha's name?" If you meditate on this topic until you understand it, then you will be enlightened. Now, if you think about The

Wonderful Dharma Lotus Flower Sutra, wondering, "How can
it be so wonderful? Why is it called "wonderful Dharma?"
What does this mean? A person who does this has drawn
near to the Buddha's wisdom. They are close to the
Buddha's wisdom, but they have not arrived at it yet.
When you arrive at it, then you truly

> deeply enter   the Sutra store
> and gain wisdom like the sea.

How does one go about "deeply entering the Sutra store?"
From the first words of The Dharma Flower Sutra, "Thus I
have heard..." you illumine the real mark of all dharmas
with your wisdom which penetrates it from beginning to
end. This doesn't mean that you merely read it by rote.
It means that you understand it and penetrate it completely. You obtain the Dharma Flower Samadhi, like the
T'ien-t'ai Master Chih-che who entered the Dharma Flower
Samadhi as he read the lines, "This is called true vigor.
This is called true Dharma offering." In this flash of
illumination, he understood the entire Sutra. True recitation of Sutras doesn't involve the mouth, and a true
offering of incense doesn't involve the hands. One of my
disciples said he couldn't recite the Shurangama Mantra,
and now he can recite it line for line. Who is reciting
it? Sutras have wonderful Dharma just like this. For
a long time he couldn't recite it, and then one day he
thought, "I should be able to do this," and he did! with-

out a single mistake. Reciting the Sutras is also this
way. The true way to recite Sutras is not with your
mouth. The true way to offer incense is not with your
hands. These are just outward ceremonies. If you obtain
the "incense offering" samadhi you can offer incense
without using your hands.

You say, "What is this Dharma Master trying to say?"

I don't know, either! Don't ask me. Not only are
you in the dark, so am I. But it doesn't seem to me
that I have said anything at all. Probably none of you
believe this.

We say that in true recitation one doesn't use the
mouth. However true recitation is not apart from the
mouth, either. Real offering of incense doesn't involve
the hands, but it's not apart from the hands, either.
One doesn't use them, and one doesn't not use them. What
is this? True recitation of Sutras is the recitation of
the wordless Sutra. The Sutra which hasn't a single
word, isn't apart from words, and it isn't apart from
"non-words." True offering of incense doesn't involve
the hands, nor is it apart from the hands. This is
because you use the heart to offer incense. In this way
you are offering incense all the time, in the six periods
of the day and night. However, the offering of incense
doesn't depend on the hand, and it isn't apart from the
hand.

Today, one of my confused disciples asked his confused teacher about a confusing situation. The confused disciple didn't understand himself. He said, "Sometimes when I talk, it's me. Other times when I talk it's not me. One person has turned into two people."

Would you call that confused? The confused teacher didn't understand what was going on, either. The confused teacher didn't want to be stuped by his confused disciple, however, so he thought of a confused solution to the problem. He said, "Don't have yourself talk and don't have the other person talk. Have the 'truth' do the talking. Whatever part is true, let that part do the talking."

The confused disciple heard this and his confused question was answered. His question was clarified by his confused teacher. Who would have guessed that a confused teacher would instruct a disciple into non-confusion?

Sutra: T. 32a18
One who speaks this sutra
Should enter the Thus Come One's room
Put on the Thus Come One's robes,
And sit on the Thus Come One's throne,
And fearlessly, in the assembly,
Expound it to them in detail.
Great compassion is the Thus Come One's room,

Gentleness and patience are the Thus Come
  One's robes,
The emptiness of all Dharmas is the Thus Come
  One's throne.
Dwelling in this, one should speak the Dharma.
If, when one speaks this sutra
Someone should slander him with evil mouth,
Or hit him with knives, sticks, tiles or stones
Recollecting the Buddha, he should endure this.

Outline:

H2.   Verse about method.
I1.   Statement of method.

Commentary:

ONE WHO SPEAKS THIS SUTRA/ to explain The Dharma
Flower Sutra after my extinction. SHOULD ENTER THE THUS
COME ONE'S ROOM/ First of all they must enter the
Buddha's room PUT ON THE THUS COME ONE'S ROBES/ AND SIT
ON THE THUS COME ONE'S THRONE/ AND FEARLESSLY, IN THE
ASSEMBLY / They should not be intimidated by the size of
the audience. EXPOUND IT TO THEM IN DETAIL/ expound
upon it broadly and in detail.

What is the Thus Come One's room? It's certainly
not the room he lives in. GREAT COMPASSION IS THE THUS
COME ONE'S ROOM/ You must have a greatly compassionate
heart and vow to save all living beings, helping them to

leave suffering, attain bliss, end birth and cast off
death, and quickly realize the Buddha Path. Compassion
means that one would not deliberately harm even a blade
of grass or a tiny bug, an ant, or a mosquito. The
purpose of Liberating Life in Buddhism is for the
nurturing compassion. If you have true compassion you
will realize that all living beings are of one substance.
Since we are all of the same substance, it's up to us to
help creatures gain their freedom. Yesterday, we liberated some pigeons. Perhaps they were your relatives,

father, mother, brothers or sisters, from former lives---
it doesn't matter--they are living beings, and they are
suffering so we should help them to gain freedom. That's
compassion. Compassion doesn't mean being compassionate
in one situation and not in another. Compassion means
a universal concern for the welfare of all creatures.
It's not partial to human beings, or animals, or any
particular form of life. Compassion should extend to all
of existence, to the entire Dharma Realm. This is the
Thus Come One's room--great compassion. GENTLENESS AND
PATIENCE ARE THE THUS COME ONE'S ROBES/ Gentleness means
that one is not violent. The Earth Store Bodhisattva
Sutra says, "Stubborn living beings are hard to subdue."
Gentleness is the opposite of toughness.

Patience is the most wonderful of Dharmas. It is
the third of the six perfections. Patience is of three
types: produced patience, dharma patience, and unproduced

dharma patience. Produced patience refers to the ability to endure both good and evil treatment by other living beings and to bear what others cannot bear. You must yield where others cannot yield. You can endure hunger, thirst, fatigue, wind, rain, heat, and cold. Cultivating patience and gentleness are like the Thus Come One's clothing.

Dharma patience means that in your investigation of the Buddhadharma you endure long periods of study. If you have no patience your mind may become uneasy and impatient. You might think, "I have studied so much Buddhadharma and read so many Sutras and learned so many mantras, but so much remains. I'll never get to the end of it." And you think about quitting.

Or perhaps you have just begun to study and you get anxious thinking, "I'll never catch up with the others," and you can't be patient. In studying the Buddhadharma you have to be patient. You can't get nervous or anxious because that's just false thinking. If you have too much false thinking, you'll forget everything you know.

There is also the unproduced Dharma patience. What is "not produced?" Ignorance is not produced. This refers to the state in which you view that within the entire three thousand great thousand worlds not a single dharma is produced or destroyed. This kind of vision is extremely hard to endure, but you can bear it. Or say your five eyes are about to open, and you have to be patient with a lot of uncomfortable states. You may get headaches or feel that you can't see anything. You must be patient, pay no attention to the discomfort. Basically, it may be impossible to bear, but you must bear it. If you can't bear it, you can't get enlightened. You must not lose patience and get nervous or upset.

THE EMPTINESS OF ALL DHARMAS IS THE THUS COME ONE'S THRONE/ Some people might get an understanding of all the Dharmas and then become self-satisfied. Take care not to do this. Don't think, "I know all about the Dharma. I can lecture The Shurangama Sutra and The Lotus Sutra and The Vajra Sutra. I am a lot more advanced than everyone else." If you think like this, you haven't seen the emptiness of all dharmas. On the contrary, you have become obstructed by the dharmas. Not only have you failed to gain any true understanding of dharmas, but you have formed an attachment to them. With such an attachment, you can't gain the throne of the Thus Come One, that is, the emptiness of all dharmas.

If one has an attachment to Dharmas, one can't obtain the emptiness of all dharmas and "sit on the throne of the Thus Come One."

Those of you who had never seen liberating life would have first impressions about it. Yesterday we liberated life, and afterwards I asked you each how you felt about it. Once it's done it's done, but still you're impressions remain.

DWELLING IN THIS, ONE SHOULD SPEAK THE DHARMA/ One shouldn't have an attachment to self and others. One should not have the mark of self, living beings, others, or a life.

IF, WHEN ONE SPEAKS THE SUTRA/ SOMEONE SHOULD SLANDER HIM WITH AN EVIL MOUTH/ Let's say right while you are lecturing someone comes along and starts yelling at you. Basically, you are doing something meritorious, but this person reviles you for it. OR HIT HIM WITH KNIVES, STICKS, TILES OR STONES/ RECOLLECTING THE BUDDHA, HE SHOULD ENDURE THIS/ Think of the Buddha's great compassion, and remain gentle and patient. Remember the emptiness of all dharmas. Since all dharmas are empty, the one hitting you is empty, and you are empty, and so what is there to make you angry? Recollect the Buddha, the Dharma, and the Sangha. Recollect the Buddha and cultivate compassion. Recollect the Dharma and cultivate patience. Recollect the Sangha and cultivate gentleness.

Sutra: T. 32 a 25
In a thousand myriads of millions of lands
I manifest a pure, solid body,
Throughout limitless millions of aeons,
Speaking Dharma for the sake of living beings.
If after my extinction,
There is one who can speak this sutra,

I will send by transformation the four assemblies,
Bhikshus and bhikshunis,
As well as men and women of purity,
To make offerings to that Dharma Master.
I will gather living beings there
To listen to the Dharma.
Should someone wish to harm him,
With knives, sticks, tiles, or stones,
I will send transformed people,
To surround and protect him.
Should the speaker of Dharma
Be alone in an uninhabited place
Where it is lonely without a human sound,
And there be reading and reciting this sutra,
I will then manifest
A pure and radiant body.
Should he forget a single passage or sentence,
I will remind him so he recites it smoothly.
Should persons of such virtue
Preach for the four assemblies,
Or recite the sutra in a deserted place,
They shall all see me.
Should one be dwelling in an empty place
I will send gods and dragon kings,

Yakshas, ghosts, spirits, and so forth
To be listeners in the Dharma assembly.
This person will delight in speaking the Dharma,
And explain it in detail without obstruction.
Because the Buddhas are protective and
mindful of him,
He can cause the assembly to rejoice greatly.

Outline:

I2. The five kinds of benefit.

Commentary:

IN A THOUSAND MYRIADS OF MILLIONS OF LANDS/ I
MANIFEST A PURE, SOLID BODY,/ Shakyamuni Buddha says,
"After I enter into Nirvana I will manifest bodies
THROUGHOUT LIMITLESS MILLIONS OF AEONS/ SPEAKING DHARMA
FOR THE SAKE OF LIVING BEINGS/ IF AFTER MY EXTINCTION/
THERE IS ONE WHO CAN SPEAK THIS SUTRA/ The Wonderful
Dharma Lotus Flower Sutra, I WILL SEND BY TRANSFORMATION
THE FOUR ASSEMBLIES/ BHIKSHUS AND BHIKSHUNIS/ AS WELL AS
MEN AND WOMEN OF PURITY/ Upasakas and Upasikas. TO
MAKE OFFERINGS TO THAT DHARMA MASTER/ to the one speaking
the Dharma. I WILL GATHER LIVING BEINGS THERE/ TO
LISTEN TO THE DHARMA/ I will gather them together to
listen to the Dharma.

SHOULD SOMEONE WISH TO HARM HIM/ To hurt the Dharma
Master WITH KNIVES, STICKS, TILES, OR STONES/ I WILL

SEND TRANSFORMED PEOPLE/TO SURROUND AND PROTECT HIM/ to
protect that person from harm.

Although Shakyamuni Buddha has entered into Nirvana,
now in other worlds and other lands, he has become a
Buddha in order to teach and transform living beings.
Now, here in this Saha world when someone speaks The
Dharma Flower Sutra, then Shakyamuni Buddha, from other
lands, is protective and mindful of that Dharma Master.
Not only does Shakyamuni mindfully protect those who
lecture on the Sutra, but he also protects those who
receive and uphold this Sutra, those who read, recite,
and write it out. This is the Dharma Master Chapter
which discusses the five types of Dharma Masters of whom
the Buddha is protective and mindful. Since Shakyamuni
Buddha can't come in person, he sends transformed people
and the gods and dragons of the eight-fold division.
There are five types of Dharma Masters protected mindfully by the Buddha, but, ultimately what is a "Dharma
Master?"

Dharma is the teaching of Shakyamuni Buddha.
Master means first of all that they take the Dharma as
their Master. It also means that they bestow the
Dharma upon others.

SHOULD THE SPEAKER OF DHARMA/ "If, after my extinction," continues the Buddha, "there is someone who wishes
to speak The Dharma Flower Sutra himself... Perhaps he
decides to do it on his own or perhaps others request him
to do it, but at any rate if he should BE ALONE IN AN

UNINHABITED PLACE/ This is a Dharma Master who decided himself to live deep in the mountains, perhaps in a cave, in a solitary place, alone WHERE IT IS LONELY WITHOUT A HUMAN SOUND/ an extremely pure place. All day long you never hear a human voice, for a whole month or even an entire year, ten years, a hundred years, you don't hear a human sound. AND THERE BE READING AND RECITING THIS SUTRA/ In such a place it is easy to enter samadhi, to gain Dhyana samadhi. Perhaps he reads it, or perhaps he recites it from memory I WILL THEN MANIFEST/ right then in this solitary place, I will appear to this culti- vator in A PURE AND RADIANT BODY/ This pure and radiant body is also just pure wisdom. Pure wisdom means no jealousy or obstruction. It is pure and light. Shakyamuni Buddha will manifest this body. What is the pure and radiant body? It is just The Dharma Flower Sutra. The Dharma Flower Sutra will cause you to give rise to pure wisdom. When you have pure wisdom, then you obtain pure light. With pure light you manifest the pure dharma body.

SHOULD HE FORGET A SINGLE PASSAGE OR SENTENCE/ I WILL REMIND HIM SO HE RECITES IT SMOOTHLY/ Perhaps in a dream I will come and tell him, "You forgot a word there. Remember to put it in." Or perhaps the Buddha will remind you when you are sitting in Dhyana samadhi and your memory lapses. "How do those verses in the Dharma Master chapter go? Let's see, 'Should the speaker

of Dharma/ Be alone in an uninhabited place/ Where it is
isolated without a human sound/...then what? Oh! I
remember: And there be reading and reciting this Sutra.'"
You will suddenly remember it. Actually it isn't you
remembering it. It's Shakyamuni Buddha in the land of
eternal quiescent light, shining his wisdom light upon
you so that you can remember it. Wouldn't you say that
was wonderful? It's even more wonderful than buying your
own computer! It's faster than a computer, and you don't
have to program it or get a print-out or anything. The
Buddha's computer is more efficient than ours!

SHOULD PERSONS OF SUCH VIRTUE/ that is people with
with pure cultivation and virtuous practice, people
without lust, greed, hate, stupidity, people who have
morality, samadhi, and wisdom. PREACH FOR THE FOUR
ASSEMBLIES/ speak The Dharma Flower Sutra OR RECITE THE
SUTRA IN A DESERTED PLACE/ THEY SHALL ALL SEE ME/ "Me"
here, just means The Dharma Flower Sutra. If you recite
The Dharma Flower Sutra and obtain the wisdom of The
Dharma Flower Sutra, then you have opened the wisdom of the
Buddha and attained a vision of the Buddha himself.
SHOULD ONE BE DWELLING IN AN EMPTY PLACE/ I WILL SEND
GODS AND DRAGON KINGS/ YAKSHAS, GHOSTS, SPIRITS, AND SO
FORTH/ TO BE LISTENERS IN THE DHARMA ASSEMBLY/ Because
there are no human beings there, the Buddha will send all
the gods and dragons, and Dharma protectors, and so forth
to be the audience. THIS PERSON WILL DELIGHT IN SPEAKING

THE DHARMA/ AND EXPLAIN IT IN DETAIL WITHOUT OBSTRUCTION/
One principle will expand into limitless meanings, and the
limitless meanings will return to the one principle. He
will be unobstructed--light upon light interpenetrating,
like Indra's net. BECAUSE THE BUDDHAS ARE PROTECTIVE
AND MINDFUL OF HIM/ of the one speaking The Dharma Flower
Sutra, HE CAN CAUSE THE ASSEMBLY TO REJOICE GREATLY/
Because the Buddha is helping this person speak the
Dharma, there isn't a single person who is unhappy. They
are all happy and delighted. Even if this Dharma Master
scolds people, they like to listen to it. Why? Because
he has virtue.

Sutra: T. 32 b 14
One who draws near this Dharma Master
Will quickly gain the Bodhisattva Path.
One who follows this master in study
Will see Buddhas as countless as the Ganges'
sands.

Outline:

G3. Concluding exhortation.

Commentary:

ONE WHO DRAWS NEAR THIS DHARMA MASTER/ Who expounds
upon The Dharma Flower Sutra WILL QUICKLY GAIN THE
BODHISATTVA PATH/ the way cultivated by the Bodhisattvas.
ONE WHO FOLLOWS THIS MASTER IN STUDY/ WILL SEE BUDDHAS

AS COUNTLESS AS THE GANGE'S SANDS/ If you study the Buddhadharma with this teacher you see countless Buddhas. The Buddhas will rub you on the crown and give you a prediction, saying "Good man, in the future you shall become a Buddha," and so on.

Do you see how inconceivable The Dharma Flower Sutra is? Today we have finished The Dharma Master Chapter.

On the first day of the Summer Session we'll start Chaper Eleven: Seeing the Jeweled Stupa. Whoever wants to see a jeweled stupa shouldn't miss it.

"What's the use of seeing a jeweled stupa?" you ask.

If you see one then you can live in one, and you won't have to worry about having no place to live!

Originally the Buddha's birthday is Tuesday, but since everyone works during the week we are having it on Sunday. If you bathe the Buddha, in the future people will come and bathe you. If you don't, when you become a Buddha no one will remember your birthday! Everything is a matter of cause and effect. Why do so many people remember Shakyamuni Buddha's birthday? It's because in limitless aeons in the past he bathed other Buddhas. Bathing the Buddha now is for the future when you become a Buddha. If you don't want to become a Buddha, you can forget about bathing the Buddha. If you don't care about the result, you don't need to plant the cause. However, if you think, "The Buddha isn't bad. He's greatly enlightened and really understands everything. I'd like to be like that," then you should join in and bathe the Buddha.

Basically, the Buddha's body is perfectly clean and he doesn't need a bath. The ceremony is a manifestation of our filial thoughts towards the Buddha. "Our teacher, Shakyamuni Buddha's birthday has come around. When he was born nine dragons came to bathe him and so we follow their example and bathe the Buddha. We are Buddhist disciples and so we should be filial to our teacher." One needn't give a lot of money in exchange for bathing the Buddha. Since, unlike some places, we don't charge money for bathing the Buddha, our ceremony is really clean. I hope this is clear now. We aren't in it for the money.

The Dharma which is transmitted here is the "everything okay" Dharma.

 **his is the eleventh of twenty-eight chapters**
of <u>The Wonderful Dharma Lotus Flower Sutra</u>.
Stupa is a Sanskrit word. It means "square
grave". It is a place where the relics of
Buddhas and patriarchs are kept so that
people can make offerings to them. They are
also places where the Buddhas'sharira are
kept. The Jeweled Stupa in this Chapter
was built by living beings for the Buddha
Many Jewels after that Buddha went to
Nirvana. Before he became a Buddha, the
Buddha Many Jewels made a vow saying,
"In the future wherever a Buddha manifests in any world and speaks <u>The Dharma</u>

Flower Sutra, my Jeweled Stupa will rise out of the earth in front of the assembly. It will appear in space so that all in the Dharma assembly can see it. When they see it, it will prove that the realm of The Dharma Flower Sutra is inconceivable." He made the vow that whenever any Buddha spoke the Sutra he would do this. Now, Shakyamuni Buddha is lecturing on The Dharma Flower Sutra and so the Thus Come One Many Jewels, based on his vow power, manifests in empty space. This should make us understand how important The Dharma Flower Sutra is. Therefore, the Buddha spoke it at the very end of his teaching career. First he spoke The Avatamsaka Sutra. Then he spoke the Agamas and the Vaipulya Sutras. Then he spoke Prajna. He waited until the very end to speak The Dharma Flower and Nirvana Sutras.

Now in America, first we lectured on The Shurangama Sutra. Last year during the summer session we spoke the Chapter of the Conduct and Vows of Universal Worthy Bodhisattva from The Avatamsaka Sutra and also The Sixth Patriarch Sutra. This year we are going to lecture this chapter of The Dharma Flower Sutra during the summer session.

We are gathered here in this lecture hall to investigate the Buddhadharma together. This is not a small causal condition, it is a great one. However, since you haven't gained the penetration of past lives or the heavenly eye, you won't understand the causes and conditions.

Now that you have the opportunity to listen to this chapter of The Dharma Flower Sutra, that's an inconceivable state manifesting.

Most people see with their eyes. We see the Jeweled Stupa not only with the eyes, but with the mind. Not only do we see it with the mind, but we see it with the original nature. This is because the Thus Come One Many Jewels is within the original nature of each one of us. The Stupa manifests from the Original Nature as the Thus Come One. Our vision of it is a vision of the Original Nature's Thus Come One. This is how we see the Jeweled Stupa. It isn't like any jeweled stupas we have ever seen. It is really big and high!

I just said that the mind and the nature see the Jeweled Stupa and some people might not believe this principle. This principle, however, is completely true. Most people just know what they see with their eyes. They don't know that, basically, the eyes don't do the seeing at all. If the seeing were in the eyes, then when people were dead, and their eyes were still there, they should still be able to see things! Why can't people see then? That proves that it isn't the eyes that see. It's the mind.

"This is the scientific age. It's possible to take the eyes from one person and transplant them in another person's body so that the second person can see," you say.

Yes, but in that case it still isn't the eyes that

see. The seeing is done by the seeing nature. Without
the seeing nature, one cannot see.

"Well, then, what does the seeing nature look like?"
you ask.

You can't see it! So The Shurangama Sutra says,
"When your seeing sees the seeing (nature),this seeing
is no (longer) seeing. Your seeing (nature) is beyond
your seeing, and your seeing cannot reach it."

"If I can't see it, then it doesn't exist!" you
say.

If you want to reason that way, then the things you
do see don't exist either!

You say, "I don't believe it."

It's just because you don't believe it that you
don't understand the doctrines contained in The Dharma
Flower Sutra.

The Dharma Flower Sutra is for the purpose of
breaking all your attachments. The material
objects you see belong to the "marks division" of the
Eighth Consciousness. In reality, they do not exist.
That which you cannot see is real.

"But if it is real, I should be able to see it,"
you say.

It's just because you are off by that much. Basically, you can see it. Your self nature is filled with
shining light, interpenetrating without obstruction. But
you mistake the false for the true and so you can't see

the true. If you put down the false, then the true will manifest. That's the real you. The Shurangama Sutra investigates the question of "seeing" in great detail. Ananda can't keep up with the Buddha's arguments, either.

We should leave all our attachments. That which you cannot see is your true seeing. That which you can see is a manifestation of the marks division of your Eighth Consciousness. The more you investigate these principles, the more wonderful they get. The Vajra Sutra says, "All that which has marks is empty and false. If you can see all marks as no marks, then you can see the Thus Come One." Can you see all marks as no marks? That means putting down the false so that the true manifests. Everything with shape and marks is false. If you see these false marks as untrue and false, then you see the Buddha.

So we will take the discussion of "seeing" the Jeweled Stupa and see it this far.

Sutra : T. 262, 32b17

At that time, there manifested before the Buddha a stupa made of the seven jewels. It was five hundred yojanas in height and two hundred and fifty yojanas in breadth. It welled up out of the earth and stood in empty space, adorned with all kinds of jeweled objects. It had five thousand railings and thousands of myriads of alcoves. Countless banners and pennants adorned it as well. Jeweled beads were hung from it and myriads of millions of jeweled bells were suspended from its top. The scent of Tamalapatracandana issued from all four sides and filled the entire world. All its banners and canopies were made of the seven jewels: gold, silver, lapis lazuli, mother of pearl, carnelian, real pearls and agate reaching up to the palace of the four heavenly kings.

Outline:

> D2. Vision of the Jeweled Stupa:
>> Chapter 11.
>>> E1. Prose.
>>>> F1. Many Jewels manifests.
>>>>> G1. The manifesting of the
>>>>> Stupa.

Commentary:

AT THAT TIME, when the Buddha had finished speaking the Dharma Master chapter, THERE MANIFESTED BEFORE THE BUDDHA A STUPA MADE OF THE SEVEN JEWELS. IT WAS FIVE HUNDRED YOJANAS IN HEIGHT AND TWO HUNDRED AND FIFTY YO-JANAS IN BREADTH. A small yojana is forty miles. A medium-sized yojana is sixty miles, and a big yojana is eighty miles. The yojanas referred to in the text are large yojanas.

Where did it come from? IT WELLED UP OUT OF THE
EARTH AND STOOD IN EMPTY SPACE, ADORNED WITH ALL KINDS
OF JEWELED OBJECTS. There were all kinds of priceless
ornaments on it. IT HAD FIVE THOUSAND RAILINGS AND THOU-
SANDS OF MYRIADS OF ALCOVES. COUNTLESS BANNERS AND PEN-
NANTS ADORNED IT AS WELL.

JEWELED BEADS WERE HUNG FROM IT. The Jeweled Stupa
was covered with strings of beads. These beads are hollow inside. In the Sutra of Sixteen Contemplations we
read about the wicked Prince Ajatashatru who put his
father, the King, in prison. The prison was inside
seven locked gates. The Prince did this at the urging
of Devadatta who said, "Shakyamuni is the old Buddha.
We should have a revolution and then I will be the new
Buddha. I will be the new Buddha, and you will be the
new King! The new King and the new Buddha together will
rule the land!" So, the Prince put the "old King" in
jail. No one was allowed to see him except his wife,
and he wasn't given any food or drink. What a crummy
son. She took her beads, which were hollow and filled
them with grape juice and smuggled them into the King's
cell.

The King was in his cell crying about his predica-
ment and lamenting the miseries of this world. Then he
prayed to the Buddha for help. "The Buddha has spiritual powers. He should come and save us." Just then
Mahamaudgalyayana manifested to rescue them. He took

them to the Jeta Grove where the Buddha spoke for them The Sutra of Sixteen Contemplations. He talked about how the world is filled with suffering, and there is nothing to hold onto. If you have given birth to a son, you shouldn't hold your expectations too high. He might disappoint you. He might even put you in jail! That's the way this world works. If you understand it, you know there's nothing to it. If you don't understand, you might think it is very fine. If you do understand it, you know it is like a dream, like an illusion. Don't look upon it as real.

The Stupa was five hundred yojanas in height. This represents being able to stop the wheel of the five paths of rebirth in which living beings suffer. The Stupa was two hundred and fifty yojanas wide. The two hundred fifty yojanas on each of its four sides represents the two hundred and fifty precepts. In cultivation, you must rely upon the power of the Precepts to accomplish the karma of the Way. There are four sides and they represent 250 Precepts in walking, 250 Precepts in standing, 250 Precepts in sitting, and 250 Precepts in reclining--the four comportments. Together they make one thousand. There are a thousand in the three periods of time--past, present, and future, and that makes three thousand. So, we say there are three thousand fine aspects of the awesome manner and eighty thousand fine practices.

The jeweled Stupa rose right out of the earth. Someone asks, "If this huge Stupa rises out of the earth, does it leave a big hole in the ground?"

This is not something we can understand with our ordinary minds. The Stupa rises out of the earth, but it doesn't leave a hole in the ground. The ground doesn't open up and let the Stupa out. It rises out of the ground very slowly. This is an inconceivable state. The Stupa was adorned with many precious objects which refers to many practices adorning one's Way karma.

"It had five thousand railings and thousands of myriads of alcoves." This represents the merit and virtue of the ten thousand good deeds.

"Countless banners and pennants adorned it as well."

The banners represent samadhi or stillness, while the pennants represent wisdom or movement. It shows the equality of samadhi and wisdom.

"Jeweled beads were hung from it." This represents the pearls of wisdom which shine brightly. Wisdom is like a jewel shining on all living beings. AND MYRIADS OF MILLIONS OF JEWELED BELLS WERE SUSPENDED FROM ITS TOP.

THE SCENT OF TAMALPATRACANDANA ISSUED FROM ALL FOUR SIDES AND FILLED THE ENTIRE WORLD. The four sides gave off the fragrance of Tamalpatracandana. Tamalpatracandana is a Sanskrit word. It means "undefiled in nature." This pure incense grows on "Ox Head Mountain." One kernel of it when burned can be smelled at a distance of forty miles. The fragrance from the Stupa filled the entire world. This represents the perfection of blessings and wisdom.

ALL ITS BANNERS AND CANOPIES WERE MADE OF THE SEVEN JEWELS. Banners and canopies represent the loftiness of the Buddhadharma. GOLD, represents the wisdom of people who have a solid resolve. SILVER is white and pure and represents purity, the cultivation of pure conduct. LAPIS LAZULI represents the
wisdom of clear understanding. MOTHER OF PEARL has what looks like cart tracks on it, which represents the ability of a true cultivator to bend to the situation, to yield and be patient. CARNELIAN is of many colors, red, yellow, white, representing the adornment of the ten thousand virtues. REAL PEARLS: Pearls are round and shining so they represent the interprenetrating, unobstructed wisdom. AGATE is a translucent stone. It appears warm and moist and represents the warm and moist wisdom. The seven jewels adorned the canopies and banners REACHING UP TO THE PALACE OF THE FOUR HEAVENLY KINGS. The Palace of the Four Heavenly Kings is half way up Mount Sumeru, not at the top of that mountain. The Buddha Stupa reached halfway up Mount Sumeru.

Sutra: T. 32 b 23

From the Heaven of the Thirty-Three there

rained heavenly mandarva flowers as an offering to the jeweled stupa. All the gods, dragons, yakshas, gandharvas, ashuras, garudas, kinnaras, mahoragas, humans, non-humans and so forth, thousands of myriads of millions of them, made offerings to the jeweled stupa of all kinds of flowers, incense, beads, banners, canopies, and instrumental music, reverently honoring it and praising it.

Outline:

G2. Offerings from the gods.

Commentary:

FROM THE HEAVEN OF THE THIRTY-THREE THERE RAINED HEAVENLY MANDARAVA FLOWERS AS AN OFFERING TO THE JEWELED STUPA. The Heaven of the Thirty-three is the Trayastrimsha Heaven, the second of the six heavens in the desire realm. It is located on the top of Mount Sumeru. There are eight heavens on each of the four sides with one in the middle making thirty-three. The ruler of this heaven is Shakra, also known in external religions as "God Almighty." Most of those in external religions do not know the origin of Shakra and think he is the highest god. In Buddhism, he is only a Dharma Protector. He doesn't even rate a seat in the Dharma Assembly, but has to stand outside the door of the Buddha's lecture hall and keep an eye on things. Each of the thirty-three heavens has its ruler who is under Shakra's command.

How did this happen? Aeons ago, after the Nirvana of Kashyapa Buddha, Shakra was a beggar-woman. One day, she came across an image of Kashyapa Buddha in an old abandoned temple and noticed that its gold finish was cracked and peeling. She gathered thirty-two of her women friends together and they pooled their savings and raised funds, and as they say, "accumulated fox-hair armpits make a coat." This phrase calls for an explanation. In northern China, it's very cold in the winter. The warmest coat you can wear, and the softest, is made up of the skin taken from the armpits of the fox. You can only get one or two inches worth of fur from each armpit, so you obviously need quite a few foxes to make a coat. In the same way it took quite a few people to gather enough resources to repair the temple. It took thirty-three, in fact, to raise pro- bably thirty thousand or so dollars. After they raised the money, they hired a carpenter to repair the temple and then they died. They died without any illness, either. They just "up and died," and--who knows quite how--they were born each in a heaven, thirty-three heavens, as rulers there. This was their reward from rebuilding the temple.

Now, we are preparing to purchase a large temple and one of the Dharma Protectors has said that he will offer up his monthly salary to meet the payments. Others

have volunteered their labor. Those who have money
should give money, and those who can work should work.
I am sure that our fox hair armpits will make up a coat,
too, and everyone will now bring forth their resolve.
You should give all you are able to give. No sense
going halfway.

"Boy, this Dharma Master is really fierce," someone is thinking.

You just figured that out? You should have known
long ago!

The rulers of the heaven of the thirty-three got
there through their merit. We shouldn't get born in
just a heaven. We can all bring forth the resolve to
build the Way Place, and then in the future we can all
be, not just heavenly rulers, but "Buddha" rulers!
That's even better! It's turning the great Dharma
Wheel. Nobody should be afraid of me. I am encouraging
you to give because I am looking out for your benefit.
I am helping you to plant good roots. This isn't to
your detriment. It's something that's really going to
help you.

This reminds me of what I used to say in Manchuria
when I was encouraging people to bring forth their
hearts to help in the work. I would say, "I have come
to your house and you should be happy. Why? Because
we are delivering the nature of Virtue and the Way to
your own house. Since we are delivering the virtue of

the Way you should plant blessings. What does that
mean? If you have money, give money. If you can work,
work. Three Conditions Temple is in the process of being built." I was not very eloquent, but whenever
these people who were probably not too bright heard
this not-too-bright person speak in this way, they would
all rush to make offerings.

"Here's thirty years of my savings!" said one.

"I am a carpenter and I will work!" said another.

People would give up their most prized attachments.
Now I have been in this country for so many years and
this is the first time I have called on you. We should
all bring forth our hearts to build the new temple. Better volunteer yourself before I "volunteer" you!

During this Summer Session we are holding a Kuan
Yin Bodhisattva Recitation Session in order to ask
Kuan Yin Bodhisattva to help those attending the session. During the first Summer Session there were great
demonic obstacles. The second Summer Session had its
share, too. I know that during this, the third session,
there will be quite a few people and a considerable
number of demonic obstacles. So we will start the session with a Kuan Yin Session and ask Kuan Yin Bodhisattva to help each of us eradicate our karmic obstacles.

I have told you before that each of us has innumer-
able karmic obstacles. Kuan Yin Bodhisattva is always
sprinkling her sweet dew, but because of the magnitude

of their karmic obstacles, people sometimes give rise
to their own mental demons. These mental demons cause
them to lose perspective and the demon takes them over.
This is a pitiful situation. It's a matter of great
concern for everyone. Those attending this Summer Session should be aware of the fact that if you want to
improve, your past offenses will attack you and try to
get in your way. If you want to become a Buddha, you
must undergo testing by the demons, too. So don't have
so much false thinking. Study the Buddhadharma with
one mind and one heart. When you listen to the Dharma
lectures, take notes. When sitting in meditation, don't
indulge in false thinking. That makes it harder for
demonic obstacles to arise. Those who haven't had demonic obstacles should help those who have. Aid them
with the power of contemplation in meditation. Help
them beat their demons back and overcome their obstacles. In this way they can, as the saying goes:

> Have a share in the true Way,
>
> And make progress in the Way,
>
> and avoid demons.

Everyone has a share in cultivation. I will be doing this sort of contemplation and all of you should,
too. Don't be turned by states.

So the text says, "From the Heaven of the Thirty-
three." The number thirty-three represents the

Ten Bodhisattva Dwellings

Ten Bodhisattva Conducts

Ten Bodhisattva Transferences

to make thirty. Then you add the Ten Grounds, counting them together as one and you get thirty-one. Then you add Equal Enlightenment and that makes thirty-two, and then Wonderful Enlightenment and you get thirty-three. These are taken from the Fifty-five Stages of Bodhisattva Development.

ALL THE GODS, DRAGONS... The gods and dragons represent the good subsidiary mind dharmas. ...YAKSHAS, GANDHARVAS, ASURAS, GARUDAS, KINNARAS, MAHORAGAS, HU-MANS, NON-HUMANS AND SO FORTH represent the evil subsidiary mind dharmas.

In his Shastra of the Door of Understanding the One Hundred Dharmas, the Bodhisattva Vasubandhu explains the One Hundred Dharmas in detail. They are divided into five general categories:

1. 11 form dharmas

2. 8 mind dharmas

3. 51 subsidiary mind dharmas

4. 24 dharmas not interactive with the mind

5. 6 unconditioned dharmas

The present analogy makes reference to the third category.

Everybody knows what dragons are, don't they? They can do all kinds of transformations; they can become big or small. They can appear and disappear. How did they get to be dragons? They are said to be "spiritual," that is, inconceivable. How did they get to be dragons, that is animals, if they have spiritual penetrations? When they were cultivating the Way, they were "quick with the Vehicle but slow with the Precepts." They cultivated the Great Vehicle Dharma with great vigor, but they did not keep the Precepts. Because they cultivated the Great Vehicle Dharma, they gained spiritual penetrations. Because they failed to keep the Precepts, they turned into animals.

Birds become birds because they are fond of "flying high," and have high ambitions. All day long they think about flying so they turn into birds.

YAKSHAS are "speedy ghosts." They get around very fast. There are ground-travelling yakshas and space-travelling yakshas. There are water-travelling yakshas, too. Speaking of yakshas, they are very fierce. Some specialize in sapping people of their energy. You may know some people who have very weak energy-systems. No matter what kind of good food they eat, they never have any energy. Most likely a yaksha ghost is busy living off of their energies. Some yakshas drink human blood, some eat people's essence. There are many varieties of yakshas.

GANDHARVAS are "incense inhaling spirits," musicians in the court of the Jade Emperor. When the Emperor

wants some music, he lights some incense and the Gandharvas all come to play.

ASURAS have big tempers. Take a look around you:
Whoever has a big temper is an asura. There are human
asuras, ghost asuras, animal asuras. Take for example
our two pigeons: Seven Bodhi Shares hasn't much of a
temper, but Twelve Links has a terrible temper. He's an
animal asura. If he gives rise to the Bodhi mind, then
he won't have such a temper, but unfortunately he is
still turning on the wheel of the "twelve links," and
so his temper remains formidable. Anger is just ignorance. The more ignorance, the more anger.

Asura is a Sanskrit word which means "ugly." It
also means "no wine." They have the blessings of the
gods but not the authority. They enjoy heavenly blessings, but they have no say in running things. Since
they have no power, they are always fighting for power,
battling with the heavenly armies.

GARUDAS are the great gold-winged-p'eng birds. They
have a wingspan of 360 yojanas. When they flap their
wings, the ocean waters part and all the dragons at the
bottom of the sea are exposed as potential meals. The
dragons have no time to transform into anything. They
are gobbled up on the spot by the Garudas, who eat them
with the same relish that we eat noodles. All gone!

The dragons were getting very upset about this, because large numbers of them were being eaten, their spe-

cies had become "endangered." They went to the Buddha
to complain and the Buddha gave them each a thread from
his precept sash, saying, "You can wear this and then
you'll be invisible to the p'eng birds!"

That worked out fine for the dragons, but the p'eng
birds were now going hungry. So they went to the Buddha
and said, "What about us? Dragons are our primary food
supply. We're going to starve!" Shakyamuni Buddha said,
"Don't worry. I'll tell all of my disciples to set out
some food for you when they eat lunch every day." That's
why left-home people send some food out for the p'eng birds.

KINNARAS are also musical spirits in the Jade Emperor's court. The Jade Emperor does a lot of entertain-
ing and always has the kinnaras play music so the gods
can dance. The gods can dance! They dance because they
are so happy they forget about everything.

MAHORAGAS are huge snakes. HUMANS, NON-HUMANS AND
SO FORTH, THOUSANDS OF MYRIADS OF MILLIONS OF THEM, MADE
OFFERINGS TO THE JEWELED STUPA OF ALL KINDS OF FLOWERS,
INCENSE, BEADS, BANNERS, CANOPIES, AND INSTRUMENTAL MUS-
IC--music of all kinds. This can also refer to disci-
plines such as yoga and the martial arts. REVERENTLY
HONORING IT AND PRAISING IT. Everyone was very respect-
ful of the Jeweled Stupa and spoke in praise of it.

Sutra: T. 32b27

At that time, a loud voice issued from the

stupa speaking in praise, saying, "Good indeed, good indeed, Shakyamuni, World Honored One that you are able, by means of your undifferentiating great wisdom, to speak for the great assembly, The Wonderful Dharma Flower Sutra, a Dharma for teaching Bodhisattvas of whom the Buddhas are protective and mindful. So it is, so it is, Shakyamuni, World Honored One, that all you say is true and real."

Outline:

> G3. The Buddha Many
> Jewels speaks in
> praise.

Commentary:

In this passage of text the Thus Come One Many Jewels certifies that Shakyamuni Buddha's speaking of The Dharma Flower Sutra is genuine and not false. AT THAT TIME, A LOUD VOICE ISSUED FROM THE STUPA SPEAKING IN PRAISE, a mighty and wonderful sound praising Shakyamuni Buddha. SAYING, "GOOD INDEED, GOOD INDEED, SHAKYAMUNI, WORLD HONORED ONE, really great, really fine! Shakya means "able to be humane." Muni means "still and silent." "Able to be humane" refers to the Buddha's compassionate rescuing of living beings. "Still and silent" refers to the accumulation of virtue gained through pure cultiva-

tion. Able to be humane refers to movement. Still and
silent refers to stillness. Within movement, there is
stillness, and within stillness there is movement. Movement does not obstruct stillness, and stillness does
not obstruct movement. Movement is stillness, and
stillness is movement. Within movement there is stillness, as stillness is the movement of non-movement.
Within stillness there is movement, as movement is the
stillness of non-stillness. Moving and yet still,
still and yet moving. Movement functions in stillness,
and stillness functions within movement. This is called
the non-dual Dharma door. Common people look upon them
as dual, but those who have opened their wisdom see
them as one. Shakyamuni Buddha, although in samadhi,
can teach all living beings. Although he is teaching
and transforming living beings, he remains in samadhi.
That's what's called "wonderful."

In case you don't understand the principle, I will
demonstrate it by means of a very simple analogy. I
know it's simple, because I understand it myself. We
can say that sleeping is just the same as being awake.
Being awake is the same as sleeping. Now, do you understand? You don't have to talk on and on about "movement
doesn't obstruct stillness, etc., etc., etc." Just remember that sleeping is waking, and waking is sleeping.
If you can feel like you are asleep when you are awake
and awake when you are sleeping, then you won't need to

sleep. Hah! The reason you feel you must sleep is because you think it's different than being awake.

"...THAT YOU ARE ABLE, BY MEANS OF YOUR UNDIFFERENTIAT-
ING GREAT WISDOM, the universal rain of your Dharma
words, TO SPEAK FOR THE GREAT ASSEMBLY THE WONDERFUL
DHARMA FLOWER SUTRA, A DHARMA FOR TEACHING BODHISATTVAS
OF WHOM THE BUDDHAS ARE PROTECTIVE AND MINDFUL. SO IT
IS, SO IT IS, SHAKYAMUNI, WORLD HONORED ONE, THAT ALL
YOU SAY IS TRUE AND REAL." It's all for real! You all
should believe it and have no doubts.

Shakyamuni Buddha was speaking the Dharma and Many
Jewels Thus Come One put in an appearance to certify to
the fact that he was right and telling the truth! So
there's your proof.

I just said that sleeping and waking were the same.
You may think of sleeping as an analogy for confusion
and waking as an analogy for enlightenment.

Now, while you are asleep are you aware of what your
activities were during the day when you were awake? Do
you still remember them? I believe most common folks
won't remember. When they are asleep they forget all
about them. In dreams, they may remember some of it,
but it's still unclear. When you are asleep, you forget about what you did yesterday, and you can't imagine
what you will be doing tomorrow. That's the way with
people in the world.

"Sometimes I have dreams and the things I dream

about actually happen to me the next day!" you say.

That's a special magical occurence, not something
you can do consciously, however. Perhaps the Buddhas
and Bodhisattvas are helping you by giving you a glimpse
into the future. That doesn't count as being your own
wisdom.

So think about it; if you can't remember what hap-
pened yesterday and you don't know what's happening tomorrow, how can you possibly expect to remember what you
did in past lives or to know what you will do in future
lives? You will be even more unclear about that. What
is more, we are as if in a dream and things are indis-
tinct. Human life is like a dream. If you can wake up
to the fact that you are dreaming, then there's some
hope for you.   Don't insist on thinking, "This
is all true. I eat and then I'm no longer hungry. This
is truly wonderful." If you think stuff like that is
"wonderful" then you won't ever discover that which is
truly wonderful. If you feel that transcendental dharmas are wonderful, you won't feel that mundane dharmas
are wonderful. It just depends on which one you pick--
the worldly or the transcendental.

Sutra: T. 32c2
Just then the four assemblies, seeing the
great jeweled stupa standing in mid-air and
hearing the voice from within it, all gained

Dharma joy and marveled at this unprece-dented occurance. They rose from their seats, revently placed their palms together and with-drew to one side.

Outline:

G4. The assembly's sur-
prise.

Commentary:

JUST THEN, right after the assembly heard the loud voice coming from the Jeweled Stupa, praising Shakyamuni Buddha, THE FOUR ASSEMBLIES, the Bhikshus, Bhikshunis, Upasakas and Upasikas... "Bhikshu" has three meanings and so it is not translated from the Sanskrit. It means "mendicant," "frightener of Mara," and "destroyer of evil." Above, a Bhikshu seeks the food of Dharma from all the Buddhas to nourish his Dharma body. Below, he seeks food from living beings to nourish the life of his wisdom. Begging for food he must beg from the rich and poor equally. What benefits does begging for food bring? It gives living beings a chance to plant bles-sings. Living beings make offerings to the Triple Jewel in order to attain blessings and virtue. Unless they make offerings to the Triple Jewel, their blessings thin out and day by day they accordingly undergo more suffer-ing. Many people don't know enough to make offerings on their own, so the Bhikshus beg for food to make them aware of this practice. Begging helps the Bhikshus to reduce their greed. It also helps laypeople give rise to charitable hearts. When Bhikshus beg, they beg in succession from one house to the next; they can't skip over the poorer families and beg from the rich, hoping for better offerings. They must not discriminate in their begging. They have to beg equally from all living beings so that all have an equal chance to plant blessings.

The second meaning of the word "Bhikshu" is frightener of Mara. When Bhikshus leave home, the heavenly demons are upset. This is like when you come here to study the Buddhadharma, the demon kings use all their tricks to get you to quit studying because they don't like it one bit. If you leave home, the demons are even more unhappy. When Bhikshus step up on the Precept Platform to receive the Precepts, the three masters and seven certifiers represent the Buddhas of the ten directions and three periods of time who administer and certify the Precepts, ask you, "Have you brought forth the Bodhi mind?" And you say, "Yes." Then they ask you, "Are you a great hero?" and you say, "Yes I am." At that time, an earth travelling yaksha takes the news to a space-travelling yaksha and the space travelling yaksha flies up to the demon kings in the heavens and informs them that, among human beings, yet another one has left home to become a Bhikshu. When the demon king hears this, his palace quakes, like an earthquake, and the demon king is afraid. Thus, Bhikshus are called "frighteners of Mara."

Thirdly, the word Bhikshu means "destroyer of evil." Bhikshus break through all the evils of afflictions. People have afflictions which come with them at birth. When they are born, they lose their tempers and get mad and cry. Bhikshus break through affliction, and just that is Bodhi. They give rise to the Bodhi mind. Since the word Bhikshu includes these three meanings, it is not translated but is left in the Sanskrit. A Bhikshuni is a woman who has left home and the same three meanings apply. An Upasaka is a layman and an Upasika is a lay-woman. The Sanskrit word Upasaka means "man who is close in work," as a layman works cloesly with the Triple Jewel. Upasika means "a woman who is close in work," working closely with the Triple Jewel. These are the four assemblies of disciples.

SEEING THE GREAT JEWELED STUPA STANDING IN MID-AIR. Our stupas are on the ground. Why was this stupa in the air? What was it standing on? What was its foundation? How could it do this?

Well, what about the space sattelites that orbit around and around? If people can invent these, how much the more so could they happen in the Buddhadharma. The Buddhadharma is a lot more subtle and wonderful than the dharmas of people. The Jeweled Stupa is sort of like a space station. There's nothing strange about the

Jeweled Stupa in space, then. This represents that the Buddha dwells nowhere and has no attachments. How can one stand still in empty space? Without attachments anywhere.

AND HEARING THE VOICE FROM WITHIN IT--they heard the wonderful, mighty voice coming from the Stupa--ALL GAINED DHARMA JOY. They were so happy, they forgot all about their troubles, AND MARVELED AT THIS UNPRECEDENTED OCCURENCE. No wonder you asked how the Stupa could stand in empty space. Even the four-fold assembly who saw it with their own eyes thought that it was strange. "Gee! How weird! How can a jeweled stupa stand there in empty space?" THEY ROSE FROM THEIR SEATS, REVER-ENTLY PLACED THEIR PALMS TOGETHER AND WITHDREW TO ONE SIDE. Because their minds were filled with awe and won-der, their bodies expressed reverence by withdrawing to one side. They stood up and withdrew because they didn't understand it. They marveled at it, and wanted Shakya-muni Buddha to answer their questions about it.

Sutra : T. 32 c 4

Just then a Bodhisattva Mahasattva by the name of Great Delight in Speaking, knowing the doubts in the minds of all the gods, humans, and asuras and others from all the worlds, spoke to the Buddha saying, "World Honored One, by *means of what causes and conditions has this jeweled stupa welled up out of the earth and produced this loud sound ?"*

Outline:

G5. The question of Great
Delight in Speaking.

Commentary:

JUST THEN A BODHISATTVA MAHASATTVA... "Bodhi" means enlightenment. "Sattva" is a sentient being. A Bodhisattva enlightens all sentient beings. A Bodhisattva is an enlightened being among sentient beings, an enlightened one. A Mahasattva is a Great Bodhisattva. This Bodhisattva is not only an enlightened one among living beings who can benefit self and others. Bodhisattvas think only to benefit others and they pay no attention to whether or not they themselves receive any benefits. They teach, transform, and rescue all living beings, causing all living beings to leave suffering and attain bliss. So they are called Great Bodhisattvas. Bodhisattvas resolve to give up their very lives for living beings. So Shakyamuni Buddha in past lives when practicing the Bodhisattva Path gave up his life over one thousand times to teach living beings. If living beings failed to respond to his teaching, he would even give up his life if necessary to save them. The Bodhisattva Path is not all that easy to practice. You all

remember the story about Shariputra who tried to practice the Bodhisattva Path, don't you? He heard the
Buddha praising the Bodhisattva Path as the highest path
and so he thought he would try it out. He was the most
intelligent of all the Buddha's disciples and he had the
best memory. However, it proved to be too much for him.
When you practice the Bodhisattva Path, take care not to
be like Shariputra!

...BY THE NAME OF GREAT DELIGHT IN SPEAKING. He
might not have been too welcome here, because he probably
talked too much. We don't talk a lot here. But, he
could come here if he wanted to. We could work it out.
KNOWING THE DOUBTS IN THE MINDS OF ALL THE GODS, HUMANS,
AND ASURAS AND OTHERS FROM ALL THE WORLDS, SPOKE TO THE
BUDDHA SAYING, "WORLD HONORED ONE, BY MEANS OF WHAT
CAUSES AND CONDITIONS HAS THIS JEWELED STUPA WELLED UP
OUT OF THE EARTH AND PRODUCED THIS LOUD SOUND?"
It went straight up into the air and a wonderful sound
came forth from it. Why? Please, teacher, be compas-
sionate and tell us. We all have doubts about this mat-
ter.

Sutra : T. 32 c7
Then the Buddha told the Bodhisattva
Great Delight in Speaking: within this jeweled
stupa is the complete body of the Thus Come One.
Long ago, limitless thousands of myriads of

millions of asankheya worlds to the east, in a land called jeweled purity, there was a Buddha by the name of Many Jewels. When this Buddha was practicing the Bodhisattva path, he made a great vow saying, "After J have become a Buddha and passed into extinction, in any of the ten direction lands where The Dharma Flower Sutra is being spoken, my stupa shall appear there, that J may hear the sutra and certify it, praising it, saying, 'Good indeed! good indeed!'"

Outline:

> G6. The Thus Come One answers.
>
> H1. Why the Stupa welled out
> of the earth.

Commentary:

THEN THE BUDDHA TOLD THE BODHISATTVA GREAT DELIGHT IN SPEAKING: Since you asked, I will tell you. WITHIN THIS JEWELED STUPA IS THE COMPLETE BODY OF THE THUS COME ONE. Which Thus Come One? LONG AGO, LIMITLESS THOUSANDS OF MYRIADS OF MILLIONS OF ASANKHYEYA WORLDS TO THE EAST, IN A LAND CALLED JEWELED PURITY, THERE WAS A BUDDHA BY THE NAME OF MANY JEWELS. WHEN THIS BUDDHA WAS PRACTICING THE BODHISATTVA PATH, before he became a Buddha, HE MADE A GREAT VOW. Those who practice the Bodhi-

sattva Path should make vows. But you shouldn't be like
one of my disciples who made a vow to become an animal
to cross over the animals! The pigeons here now probably made such a vow in the past! At any rate, I
changed his vow to "become a living being," making it
not quite so specific. That's why you need a teacher!
So when you make vows he can change them for you! Hah!

"SAYING, "AFTER I..." He, too, uses the word "I," but
his "I" is not a selfish one. It is the "I" of "no I."
"...HAVE BECOME A BUDDHA AND PASSED INTO EXTINCTION, entered into Nirvana, IN ANY OF THE TEN DIRECTION LANDS
WHERE THE DHARMA FLOWER SUTRA IS BEING SPOKEN..." The Dharma Flower Sutra was Many Jewels Buddha's favorite Sutra.
He felt it was the most wonderful and inconceivable of
all Sutras and so he wanted to make a wonderful vow.
He said, "After I go to Nirvana, and people make me a
stupa, MY STUPA SHALL APPEAR THERE, where the Sutra is
being spoken,THAT I MAY HEAR THE SUTRA AND CERTIFY IT,
PRAISING IT, SAYING, 'GOOD INDEED! GOOD INDEED! Fantas-
tic! Someone's lecturing The Lotus Sutra here. Great!
I can hear it again.'" That was his wonderful vow. Now,
Shakyamuni Buddha is speaking about the vow he made lim-
itless, uncountable aeons ago. And now Many Jewels
Buddha is manifesting and exclaiming, "Great, great!
Wow, I made it to another Dharma Flower Sutra Assembly!"

Sutra: T. 32 c 14

After that Buddha had realized the Way, when he was about to enter into extinction, in the great assembly of gods and humans he spoke to the Bhikshus saying, "After my extinction, those who wish to make offerings to my complete body should build a large stupa."

Outline:

H2. The cause of the Stupa.

Commentary:

Because of the vow he had made when practicing the Bodhisattva Path, later AFTER THAT BUDDHA, Many Jewels, HAD REALIZED THE WAY, WHEN HE WAS ABOUT TO ENTER INTO EXTINCTION, into Nirvana, IN THE GREAT ASSEMBLY OF GODS AND HUMANS HE SPOKE TO THE BHIKSHUS SAYING... Bhikshus, Bhikshunis, Upasakas, and Upasikas are the Four-fold assembly. Some may think that after Many Jewels became a Buddha he didn't speak the Dharma and so he made a vow to protect the Buddhas who spoke The Dharma Flower Sutra. That explanation is not necessarily correct because here the text says, "Bhikshus" and Bhikshus are the ones he crossed over by speaking the Dharma to them. When he was about to enter Nirvana he told them "AFTER MY EXTINCTION, THOSE WHO WISH TO MAKE OFFERINGS TO MY COMPLETE BODY SHOULD BUILD A LARGE STUPA. Using the seven gems, one should make a big stupa.

Sutra: T. 32 c 16

By the power of his spiritual penetrations and his vow, throughout the ten direction worlds wherever anyone speaks The Dharma Flower Sutra that Buddha's jeweled stupa containing his complete body wells up from the earth before the one speaking and expresses praise by saying, "Good indeed! Good indeed!"

Great Delight in Speaking! Because he has heard The Dharma Flower Sutra being spoken, the stupa of the Thus Come One Many Jewels has now welled up out of the earth with these words of praise, "Good indeed! Good indeed!"

Outline:

> H3. The reason for the sound.

Commentary:

BY THE POWER OF HIS SPIRITUAL PENETRATIONS AND HIS VOW... Having given instructions to his disciples to build him a jeweled stupa, he uses his inconceivable spiritual penetrations and his inconceivable vows THROUGHOUT THE TEN DIRECTION WORLDS. The ten direction worlds include the four cardinal points, the intermediary points, the zenith and the nadir. In each of the ten direction worlds, however, there are hundreds of thousands of myriads of worlds, too. In each of those limitless, limitless worlds, WHEREVER ANYONE SPEAKS THE DHARMA FLOWER SUTRA... It doesn't matter where, just so a Buddha has appeared there and is speaking The Dharma Flower Sutra. THAT BUDDHA'S JEWELED STUPA CONTAINING HIS COMPLETE BODY WELLS UP FROM THE EARTH BEFORE THE ONE SPEAKING. Even though he entered Nirvana so long ago, the entire body of Many Jewels Thus Come One still manifests in the Stupa AND EXPRESSES PRAISE of the Buddha who is speaking The Dharma Flower Sutra, BY SAYING, "GOOD INDEED! GOOD INDEED! Great! I have now once again met up with the World Honored One speaking The Dharma Flower Sutra."

"GREAT DELIGHT IN SPEAKING! I will tell you, BECAUSE HE HAS HEARD THE DHARMA FLOWER SUTRA BEING SPOKEN, THE STUPA OF THE THUS COME ONE MANY JEWELS HAS NOW WELLED UP OUT OF THE EARTH. He wants to come and listen to it WITH THESE WORDS OF PRAISE, "GOOD INDEED! GOOD INDEED! Really good! Another chance to hear The Dharma Flower Sutra." He says "Good indeed!" twice, and that's the big sound from inside the Stupa.

Sutra: T. 32c20

Just then, the Bodhisattva Great Delight in Speaking, by means of the spiritual power of The Thus Come One, spoke to the Buddha saying, "World Honored One, we all wish to see this Buddha's body."

Outline:

> > F2. The division bodies gather
> > from afar.
> >
> > > G1. Great Delight in Speak-
> > > ing asks to see Many Jewels.

Commentary:

JUST THEN, THE BODHISATTVA GREAT DELIGHT IN SPEAK-
ING, BY MEANS OF THE SPIRITUAL POWER OF THE THUS COME
ONE... The Bodhisattva asks the Buddha, but why does the
text say "by means of the spiritual power of the Thus
Come One?" Why isn't it by means of his own power? It
is because, in this Dharma Assembly, all the states that
appear are manifestations of the Buddha's awesome spiritual power. Even this Bodhisattva's questions about
the doctrine come about through the aid of the Buddha's
spiritual power, lending him the wisdom so that he can
ask these questions. ...SPOKE TO THE BUDDHA SAYING,
"WORLD HONORED ONE, Shakyamuni Buddha, WE ALL WISH TO
SEE THIS BUDDHA'S BODY." The Bodhisattva Great Delight
in Speaking had heard the great sounds of praise coming from the Stupa for Shakyamuni Buddha, but he still
hadn't seen the Buddha inside the Stupa. He could only
hear him. He hadn't seen that Buddha's thirty-two
marks and eighty minor characteristics and so he was,

frankly, curious. Actually, it was the Buddha's spiritual power that caused him to ask. His question was asked on behalf of all; they all had doubts. "Such a great sound out of that Stupa! Is there a public address system in it? Is there a radio in it? Is there really a Buddha in there? We want to see that Buddha! Is that Buddha a special type of Buddha?" The gods had a lot of doubts, and they didn't know for sure if there really was a Buddha in there. The Bodhisattva Great Delight in Speaking, because he loved to talk, asked Shakyamuni Buddha to tell him about it.

They were all like children who, overhearing their parents talk about a guest who is coming, want to know all about him. "We want to see him too! We want to see the guest!"

Sutra: T; 32 c 22

The Buddha told the Bodhisattva Mahasattva Great Delight in Speaking: The Buddha Many Jewels has made a profound and solemn vow : "When my jeweled stupa manifests in the presence of the Buddhas because The Dharma Flower Sutra is heard, if there is anyone who wishes me to show my body to the four assemblies, then the division body Buddhas of that Buddha who is speaking Dharma in the worlds of the ten directions, must all return and gather together in one place. Afterward, my body will appear.

"Great Delight in Speaking, my division body Buddhas present in the ten direction worlds speaking Dharma, should now gather together."

Outline:

> G2. The division bodies
>
> should gather together.

Commentary:

THE BUDDHA, Shakyamuni, TOLD THE BODHISATTVA MAHA-
SATTVA GREAT DELIGHT IN SPEAKING: THE BUDDHA MANY
JEWELS HAS MADE A PROFOUND AND SOLEMN VOW! You want
to see the Buddha Many Jewels, but there is a condition.
In a life long ago, before he became a Buddha, he made
a very solemn vow. It is very wonderful. He said,
"WHEN MY JEWELED STUPA MANIFESTS IN THE PRESENCE OF THE
BUDDHAS BECAUSE THE DHARMA FLOWER SUTRA IS HEARD, IF
THERE IS ANYONE WHO WISHES ME TO SHOW MY BODY TO THE
FOUR ASSEMBLIES, if there are those who wish to see me,
THEN THE DIVISION BODY BUDDHAS OF THAT BUDDHA WHO IS
SPEAKING DHARMA IN THE WORLDS OF THE TEN DIRECTIONS..."
The Buddha speaking The Dharma Flower Sutra has division
bodies who are in the ten directions speaking Dharma,
too. Division bodies are transformation bodies. Shak-

yamuni Buddha has a hundred thousand myriads of millions of transformation bodies. Not only does Shakyamuni Buddha have them, but all the Buddhas have them and they are the Dharma. Their division-body Buddhas speaking Dharma in the ten directions teaching and transforming living beings, MUST ALL RETURN AND GATHER TOGETHER IN ONE PLACE." That's Many Jewels Buddha's vow. All the transformation Buddhas returning to Shakyamuni Buddha is just the ten thousand returning to the one root. The root can transform into a myriad transformations and the myriads all return to the one root. One Buddha can manifest limitless transformation Buddhas all of whom return to the one Buddha. How could common folks possibly understand such a state? That's why this Sutra is called The Wonderful Dharma Lotus Flower Sutra. It is so wonderful people couldn't possibly figure it out!

"AFTERWARD MY BODY WILL APPEAR, when all those Buddhas gathered in one place, then I will manifest. GREAT DELIGHT IN SPEAKING, MY DIVISION BODY BUDDHAS PRESENT IN THE TEN DIRECTION WORLDS SPEAKING DHARMA SHOULD NOW GATHER TOGETHER."

Sutra: T. 32 c 27

Great Delight in Speaking said to the Buddha, "World Honored One, we also wish to see the division bodies of the World Honored One so that we may bow to them and make offerings."

1698

Outline:

> G3. Great Delight in Speaking
> requests a view of the gather-
> ing.

Commentary:

When the Bodhisattva Great Delight in Speaking heard about the inconceivable vows made by the Buddha Many Jewels in the past, GREAT DELIGHT IN SPEAKING SAID TO THE BUDDHA, "WORLD HONORED ONE, WE, the gods and humans here along with the great Bodhisattvas and the four-fold assembly of disciples, not only wish to see the body of Many Jewels Buddha, but ALSO WISH TO SEE THE DIVISION BODIES OF THE WORLD HONORED ONE, Shakyamuni Buddha. Since they are all getting together, we would like to see them SO THAT WE MAY BOW TO THEM AND MAKE OFFERINGS."

What is meant by "bow?" It means to make obeisance to the Buddha. Some people say, "Buddha images are made of wood, clay, gold, silver, bronze, or iron and it is superstitious to bow to them. Since people made them in the first place, what good does it do to bow to them? What use is it? It's just superstition!"

It most certainly is _not_ superstitious. We bow to the Buddhas first of all to help get rid of our arrogance. Secondly, it causes us to give rise to a yielding and gentle mind, so that we aren't tough and stubborn. It also makes us reverent. The Buddha became a Buddha and people bow to him. Before he became a Buddha, he bowed to other Buddhas. Shakyamuni Buddha in a former life was a Bodhisattva called "Never-Slighting" and whenever he saw someone he would bow to them and say, "I dare not slight you because you will, in the future, become a Buddha." After Shakyamuni Buddha realized Buddhahood, a lot of people bowed to the Buddha. If you don't want to become a Buddha, but would rather be a hungry ghost or an animal, then don't bother to bow to the Buddha. Some people think it might be nice to be a dog and have someone take care of them and feed them; then they wouldn't have to do any work. Some people would even rather be a pig, and gets lots to eat! But such opinions are a bit too "smart." They are so smart, in fact, that they are stupid! If you want to be an animal or a ghost, then you don't need to bow to the Buddha. But if you want to become a Buddha, then you should bow to the Buddha. It is said,

> To bow once to the Buddha
> Wipes away offenses like Ganges'
> sands.

It wipes away your offense karma from limitless aeons past, the heavy offenses of birth and death. If you don't bow to the Buddha, then when you become a Buddha no one will bow to you! Recently, one of my disciples complained that none of his students would listen to him. I said, "You can't blame them. You never listened to your teacher, you know. It's not surprising at all that they don't listen to you." But it's a hard lesson. I hope that all of you will follow instructions. Then in the future when you are teachers, your students will listen to you.

"I don't want to be a teacher," you say. "I'll just be an independent Arhat."

If you don't want to be a teacher, there's really nothing to say. But if you do, then pay attention to the rules.

When you bow to the Buddha, you are bowing to the Buddha of your own self-nature. In the future, when you become a Buddha you realize the Buddhahood of your own self-nature.

"...AND MAKE OFFERINGS." This is very important. One makes offerings to the Triple Jewel, the Buddha, the Dharma, and the Sangha.

One might think, "Why should one make offerings to the Triple Jewel? Wouldn't it be a better deal if the Triple Jewel made offerings to me?"

You may think it's a bargain, but you would really be getting the short end. Why, now, do you have such poor luck? It's because in the past you didn't make offerings to the Triple Jewel. Why are you always short of money--no money for some nice clothes or a decent place to live? It's because you didn't make offerings to the Triple Jewel. As a consequence, day by day your blessings grow thinner. If you make offerings to the Triple

Jewel, your blessings will grow day by day. The Triple Jewel is the field of goodness and blessings for living beings. It is a place where living beings can plant blessings. There's a saying that goes:

Although a clay dragon can't bring rain,

If you want rain, you must seek it from a

clay dragon.

Although the Common Sangha can't bring blessings,

If you seek blessings, you must seek them

from the Common Sangha.

In China, when they need rain, they go to a Dragon King Temple and seek from the clay dragons. Usually it works! Probably you don't have this custom in the West. You may think, "It would have rained anyway!" But do you know for sure? Just how do you know it doesn't work? Your skepticism involves just as much guesswork as others' belief, you know. The ordinary members of the Sangha, that is, those who haven't certified to the fruit, can't bring blessings. However, if you are seeking blessings, you must seek them from the Common Sangha. People who have a lot of blessings in this life have gained them because in the past they made offerings to the Triple Jewel. People are poor because they did not make offerings to the Triple Jewel.

"I'm not so sure I believe this," you say.

Okay, but next life you'll still be poor! It's your choice.

1702

Sutra: T. 32c29

At that time the Buddha emitted a white-hair mark light in which were seen the Buddhas of the lands in the eastern direction equal in number to the grains of sand in five hundred myriads of millions of nayutas of Ganges rivers. All the Buddhalands had crystal for soil, and were adorned with jeweled trees and jeweled clothing. Countless thousands of myriads of millions of Bodhisattvas filled them. They were covered with jeweled canopies and jeweled nets. The Buddhas in those lands with a great and wonderful sound, were speaking the Dharma . Also seen were limitless thousands of myriads of millions of Bodhisattvas filling those lands speaking the Dharma for the multitudes. Thus it was also in the south, west, north, the four intermediate directions, as well as up and downward wherever the white hair-mark light shone.

Outline:

G4. Emitting a light which shines afar.

Commentary:

Not only did the Bodhisattva Great Delight in Speak-

ing want to see Many Jewels Buddha, but he wanted to
see all the transformations of Shakyamuni Buddha. AT
THAT TIME THE BUDDHA, Shakyamuni, EMITTED A WHITE HAIR-MARK
LIGHT. This hair-mark light is emitted from between
the Buddha's eyebrows. When it is emitted it is very
subtle, but extremely brilliant. ...IN WHICH WERE SEEN
THE BUDDHAS OF THE LANDS IN THE EASTERN DIRECTION EQUAL
IN NUMBER TO THE GRAINS OF SAND IN FIVE HUNDRED MYRIADS
OF MILLIONS OF NAYUTAS OF GANGES RIVERS. It didn't shine
into just one or two lands, but into limitless, uncountable, nayutas of worlds.

ALL THE BUDDHALANDS HAD CRYSTAL FOR SOIL--crystal
represents light, wisdom light--AND WERE ADORNED WITH
JEWELED TREES AND JEWELED CLOTHING. Jeweled Trees make
living beings feel refreshed and shaded with protection.
Jeweled clothing refers to patience and compliance.
COUNTLESS THOUSANDS OF MYRIADS OF MILLIONS OF BODHISAT-
TVAS FILLED THEM. What are the Bodhisattvas? They are
just those who give rise to the Bodhi mind in every
thought. THEY WERE COVERED WITH JEWELED CANOPIES AND
JEWELED NETS. The nets refer to the cultivation of the
Precepts. THE BUDDHAS IN THOSE LANDS WITH A GREAT AND
WONDERFUL SOUND WERE SPEAKING THE DHARMA . ALSO SEEN
WERE LIMITLESS THOUSANDS OF MYRIADS OF MILLIONS OF BOD-
HISATTVAS FILLING THOSE LANDS SPEAKING THE DHARMA FOR
THE MULTITUDES. THUS IT WAS ALSO IN THE SOUTH, WEST,
NORTH, THE FOUR INTERMEDIATE DIRECTIONS, AS WELL AS UP

AND DOWNWARD, WHEREVER THE WHITE HAIR-MARK LIGHT SHONE.

Sutra: T; 33 a 7

At that time all the Buddhas of the ten directions addressed the host of Bodhisattvas saying, "Good men! We should now go to the saha world, to the place of Shakyamuni Buddha and make offerings to the stupa of the Thus Come One Many Jewels."

Outline:

> G5. All the Buddhas come
> together.

Commentary:

AT THAT TIME, when all the limitless nayutas of worlds in the ten directions Buddhas, ALL THE BUDDHAS OF THE TEN DIRECTIONS ADDRESSED THE HOST OF BODHISATTVAS, SAYING, "GOOD MEN! WE SHOULD NOW GO TO THE SAHA WORLD, TO THE PLACE OF SHAKYAMUNI BUDDHA AND MAKE OFFERINGS TO THE STUPA OF THE THUS COME ONE MANY JEWELS. The time is ripe!" "Saha" is a Sanskrit word which means "endurable." Living beings are able to endure the sufferings of the Saha World. There are a great many varieties of suffering in this world. There are the three sufferings, the eight sufferings, and all the limitless sufferings.

The three sufferings are:

1. The suffering within suffering. This is suffering on top of suffering. For example, someone is poor and has no clothes to wear and lives in an old shack. Then a rainstorm comes up and blows his house away! He may have been suffering before, but now he is suffering even more! He lacks the three most basic necessities of life: clothing, food, and shelter.

2. The suffering of decay. Suppose someone is very well off. He has plenty of clothes and food and lives in a big, fine place. But then his house and all his valuable possessions burn up. That's the suffering of decay.

"Well, I'm not poor and I'm not rich either. So I don't suffer, then, do I?" you ask.

Even if you don't have the suffering of poverty or the suffering of decay, there is still the third kind of suffering:

3. The suffering of process. This is the suffering of the life process as one goes from childhood to middle age, to old age, and then to death. In every thought there is change, and you are not in control of it at all. Your fate controls you. It makes the child grow up and get old, and then die. You obey fate's commands to the letter. You obey the commands of fate better than the commands of your teacher. Your teacher tells you not to smoke or drink or take drugs, but you go off and do

it in secret! Boy! But when King Yama tells you it's
time to die, you are very compliant and die! That's the
suffering of process. If dying was just a matter of taking your last breath and leaving, it wouldn't be that
bad. Most people, however, get sick first, then they
die, and that is very uncomfortable. Again, if it was
just a matter of being sick for a few days, that would
be tolerable. But some people get paralyzed--half of
them dies first. Half of them refuses to listen to orders. They can't sit up or turn over or walk. How much
pain do you think that is?

There are also eight sufferings:

1. The suffering of birth. Obviously, everyone gets
born. But you forget how painful it is! When a child
is born it undergoes a lot of suffering, and so it cries.
It is said that birth is as painful as ripping the shell
off of a live turtle.

2. The suffering of old age. One's eyes go bad, one
loses one's hearing. Someone says, "Would you like a
cookie?" and you say, "No thanks, I don't want any tea."
or "Would you like some tea?" and you say, "I'm full!"
It gets real frustrating. Someone says, "How are your
children?" and you say, "My husband died long ago." They
see your lips moving, but they get the message wrong. If
that wasn't bad enough, their teeth start hurting and
fall out and then nothing tastes good when they eat it.

3. The suffering of sickness. Before you die, you

get sick.

4. The suffering of death. Death is as painful as skinning a live cow!

5. The suffering of being separated from what one loves. It is very painful when someone you love leaves you.

6. The suffering of being near those you hate. People you can't stand are always close by. The less you like them, the closer they try to get! You may move somewhere else hoping to get away from them and sure enough you meet someone even worse than they are!

7. The suffering of not getting what one wants. You may wish for wealth, fame, or profit and not get them. In general, not getting what you want is suffering.

8. The suffering of the raging blaze of the five skandhas. Form, feeling, perception, impulses and consciousness are like a raging fire. They turn you upside down.

Actually, there are limitless kinds of suffering, but there is no way you could speak of them all. Beings in this Saha World must undergo these sufferings. That is why it is called "endurable." Basically, it's unbearable, but beings somehow get through it.

The Buddhas are headed to the Saha World to make offerings to the Stupa of the Thus Come One Many Jewels. In the past he made a vow that he would appear in his Stupa wherever The Dharma Flower Sutra was being spoken.

Because Shakyamuni Buddha is speaking the Sutra, the Stupa is there.

Why did Shakyamuni Buddha leave the home life to cultivate the Way? It was because he saw all the sufferings in the world. Sufferings are endless. Seeing the sufferings of birth, sickness, old age and death, he decided to find a way to end suffering. That is why he left the home life, cultivated, and realized Buddhahood. When he became a Buddha, he truly put suffering to an end and gained true happiness.

During the Liang Dynasty Dhyana Master Pao-chih lived. He understood cause and effect well. One night a monk in a monastery heard the sound of a child crying. He went outside and saw a child in a bird's nest. The old dhyana master managed to keep him. The two bird parents couldn't get the child back. The child grew up to look like a person, but he had bird claws instead of hands! As a child, Master Pao-chih worked hard at his cultivation. It is very easy for children to get enlightened. He got the five eyes and six spiritual penetrations and became a well-respected high monk. At the time of the Emperor Wu of Liang, when there were important family occasions, people would ask monks to recite the Sutras. Someone asked Dhyana Master Pao-chih to recite at a wedding. He took one look at the gathering and said:

Strange indeed, strange, indeed!

The grandson marries the grandmother!

How could this be? Before she died, the grandmother had held her little grandson's hand and said, "All my affairs are taken care of and all my children have settled down. But who will take care of my little grandson? I can't put him down." With this one thought, she died and went to see King Yama. King Yama said, "Such emotions! Okay, you can go back and be your grandson's wife! Help him take care of things." She was reborn as a little girl, grew up, and married him. Take a look at the wheel of rebirth! The grandson marries his grandmother! All because of "leftover love."

Then Dhyana Master took a look in the kitchen and said:

The daughter eats her mother's flesh!

The little girl was sampling some pickled pig's feet, and Dhyana Master Pao-chih could see that the pig had been her mother in a former life.

The little boy beats on his father's skin.

There in the band was a drummer beating on the skin of an animal that had, in a former life, been his own father!

Pigs and sheep are sitting on the couch.

When Dhyana Master Pao-chih looked at the sofa, he saw people that had in former lives been pigs and sheep and were now the relatives who had come to congratulate the happy couple. The present set of relatives were at one time animals that had been eaten and now had returned.

The six relatives are cooking in the

pot.

The relatives in former lives had been reborn as animals and were being stewed in the pot.

Everyone comes to congratulate.

But I see that it's really suffering!

What do you think? Is it suffering? If you understand that it is suffering, then you should hurry up
and cultivate. If you don't think it's suffering, then
just turn around a few more times on the wheel of rebirth, and we'll talk about it more later.

Sutra : T. 33 a 9

*Just then the saha world was transformed
into one of purity, with lapis lazuli for soil and
adorned with jeweled trees. Its eight roads were
bordered with golden cords. In it there were
no towns, villages, cities, oceans, rivers, streams,
mountains, brooks, forests or thickets. Precious
incense was burned and mandarava flowers
completely covered the ground. Above it were
spread jeweled nets and banners hung with
jeweled bells. Only those in the assembly remained, as the gods and humans had been
moved to another land.*

Then all of the Buddhas, each bringing with him one great Bodhisattva as an attendant, reached the saha world and went to the foot of a jeweled tree. Each jeweled tree was five hundred yojanas in height and adorned with branches, leaves, flowers and fruits. Beneath each jeweled tree was a lion throne five hundred yojanas in height adorned with great jewels. Then each of the Buddhas sat in the lotus posture on his own throne.

In this way, by turns, the lands of the three thousand great thousand world were filled, and still there was no end to the division bodies of Shakyamuni Buddha from even one direction.

Outline:

> G6. Purifying the worlds.
>> H1. Purifying the Saha World.

Commentary:

In this section of text, Shakyamuni Buddha purifies the worlds three times. This is the first, purifying the Saha World.

JUST THEN, right after all the division bodies of

Shakyamuni Buddha of the ten directions said that they
wanted to go to the Saha World to make offerings to the
Stupa of the Thus Come One Many Jewels, Shakyamuni Buddha used the power of his spiritual penetrations to
transform the Saha World. THE SAHA WORLD WAS TRANS-
FORMED INTO ONE OF PURITY. Saha World is one of five
turbidities. Basically, having become a Buddha, the
Buddha dwelt in the Adorned Land of Real Reward. That
is where the Buddhas and great Bodhisattvas live. Originally, our Saha World has lapis lazuli for soil.
There are no mountains, rivers, and so forth, it's all
level and flat; but to teach living beings, Shakyamuni
manifests the marks of defilment and purity. Thus,
there is the pure land, and the defiled land of the five
turbidities.   Now, Many Jewels Thus Come One has manifested and all the transformation bodies of Shakyamuni
Buddha are going to gather together in one place. This
is like inviting an important guest to a meeting or a
party. The first thing we do is clean house and adorn
it very nicely in preparation, so the guest will be happy. Since Shakyamuni Buddha has asked his transformation bodies to gather together, he has first turned the
Saha World into a pure world. This is the first of
three such transformations that he makes.

   ...WITH LAPIS LAZULI FOR SOIL AND ADORNED WITH JEWELED
TREES. The jeweled trees are the kings of trees, like
the Bodhi tree. ITS EIGHT ROADS WERE BORDERED WITH

GOLDEN CORDS. The eight roads represent the Eightfold Path. IN IT THERE WERE NO TOWNS, VILLAGES, CITIES... These represent gatherings of men and women. In this pure world there were only men, no women. ...OCEANS, RIVERS, STREAMS, MOUNTAINS, BROOKS, FORESTS OR THICKETS. PRECIOUS INCENSE WAS BURNED. The precious incense refers to people's merit and virtue. AND MANDARAVA FLOWERS COMPLETELY COVERED THE GROUND. Mandarava flowers are the flowers that "go along with one's wish." As soon as you see these flowers, you are extremely happy. The flowers covered the ground everywhere. ABOVE IT WERE SPREAD JEWELED NETS AND BANNERS HUNG WITH JEWELED BELLS. ONLY THOSE IN THE ASSEMBLY REMAINED, AS THE GODS AND HUMANS HAD BEEN MOVED TO ANOTHER LAND. Only those in the Dharma Assembly remained. All the gods and people were relocated in another world! See, living beings can be moved to another world and not even realize it!

THEN, ALL OF THE BUDDHAS, EACH BRINGING WITH HIM ONE GREAT BODHISATTVA AS AN ATTENDANT, REACHED THE SAHA WORLD AND WENT TO THE FOOT OF A JEWELED TREE. EACH JEWELED TREE WAS FIVE HUNDRED YOJANAS IN HEIGHT AND ADORNED WITH BRANCHES, LEAVES, FLOWERS AND FRUITS. The trees were extremely beautiful. BENEATH EACH JEWELED TREE, jeweled Bodhi trees, WAS A LION THRONE FIVE HUNDRED YOJANAS IN HEIGHT ADORNED WITH GREAT JEWELS. THEN EACH OF THE BUDDHAS SAT IN THE LOTUS POSTURE ON HIS OWN THRONE.

IN THIS WAY, BY TURNS, THE LANDS OF THE THREE THOU-
SAND GREAT THOUSAND WORLDS WERE FILLED, AND STILL THERE
WAS NO END, they went on forever. How many Buddhas would
you say there were? ...TO THE DIVISION BODIES OF SHAK-
YAMUNI BUDDHA FROM EVEN ONE DIRECTION. There were Buddhas who had no place to sit, even though the entire
three thousand great thousand worlds had been filled.
And that's only the Buddhas from one direction, from the
east, that we are talking about! Standing room only!

Someone is wondering just what is meant by a Lion
Throne. The Lion Throne is the seat the Buddha sits on
when he speaks the Dharma. We call it the Lion Throne
because the Buddha speaks the Dharma like the roar of the
lion. The lion is the king of beasts and when the lion
roars the animals are all afraid. In his Song of Enlightenment the Great Master Yung-chia wrote:

The roar of the lion is the Fearless One speaking.
When the wild beasts hear it, their heads
        split open.
Elephants run wild and lose their decorum,
But the gods and dragons hear it in silence
        and rejoice.

When the lion roars, all the animals are scared to death!
Elephants are basically very strong, but when they hear
the lion roar they are subdued. The gods and dragons
hear it and are delighted.

The lotus posture is the position the Buddha is sit-

ting in, with his legs crossed in full lotus. It is also
called the Vajra position. What advantage does it have?
It is used for subduing demons. Most especially for those
who sleep sitting up, it's best to sit in lotus posture.
In this way you can subdue your mind and prevent it from
becoming scattered. In China they have the saying:

Gold Mountain legs.

That's because at Gold Mountain Monastery in China, they
didn't allow people to take their legs out of lotus posture. If you tried you would get hit. No matter how much
they hurt you had to bear it. After a while your legs
get very reliable and good for sitting. They also say:

Kao-min incense.

At Kao Min Monastery the incense would be lit for the
duration of a sit and it would never vary by even a min-
ute. Their schedule was the tightest one around.

And chatter at Hai Chao Monastery.

At Hai Ch'ao Monastery people talked all the time.

Seated in the Lotus Position it is very easy to enter samadhi, if you bear the pain, that is. Don't be
afraid of the pain like a little child who starts crying and calling for its mama. We should be great heroes.
The more it hurts, the more we have to bear up. The best
is to look into your hua t'ou. The Japanese look into the
word "無-wu," which means "nothing." Chinese will often
investigate the word "誰-shui" which means "who." They
investigate "Who is reciting the Buddha's name?" Others

may investigate the question, "Before my parents gave birth to me, what was my original face?"

There are no fixed dharmas and there is no certain way you have to investigate. It's not easy. People may investigate their hua-t'ou's for years and not find an answer to them. If the Japanese investigate "nothing," you can investigate "something!" Everything in the world can be reduced to nothing. What cannot? Look for it.

What use is investigating "nothing?" If everything is nothing then what is something? Everything comes to an end. What does not? Look for it! If you can find it, you become enlightened. If you find that thing which really cannot be reduced to nothing, just that is enlightenment. If you find out what your original face was before your parents gave birth to you, then you will become enlightened. If you find out who is reciting the Buddha's name, you will become enlightened, too. But you must really find out. You can't just fake it. That's useless. You can't just repeat things other people said, either.

The lotus posture, in Buddhism, is called the vajra jeweled sitting. If you can sit in lotus, all the gods will protect you, saying, "This person is sitting in lotus and isn't afraid of the pain. He has made it through the pain barrier. He must have a heart of the Way. We should protect him." If you can sit in lotus, wherever you go, just sit in lotus and close your eyes, and--at least in China--people will make offerings to you. But you shouldn't sit in lotus just to get offerings! You should sit in lotus because cultivators should sit that way, that's all. You shouldn't sit there in lotus with a sign that advertises your superior cultivation. If you are going to sit in lotus just to get offerings, you would be better off to forget the whole thing. Go get a job. You'll make more money that way. Offerings will just keep you alive. You won't get rich that way, believe me. But if you really want to get enlightened and become a Buddha, then you should definitely learn to sit that way. So I have taken this time to explain to you what sitting in lotus means.

In investigating the hua-t'ou don't investigate "something" or "nothing."

"Then what should I do?" you ask.

Don't be nervous! In the writings of other religions they begin with either "nothing" or "something." They figure that everything is either existent or non-existent and nothing goes beyond these two. We shouldn't investigate either one. We should investigate that which is neither "something" nor "nothing."

What neither is nor is not? What is neither form nor emptiness? What is neither right nor wrong, neither defiled nor pure? What neither comes nor goes? You should apply your effort here: "Nothing" is true emptiness.

"Something" is wonderful existence. True emptines is not empty, and wonderful existence is non-existence. True emptiness is not empty and so it contains wonderful existence. Wonderful existence is non-existence and so it contains true emptiness. True emptiness and wonderful existence are "two and yet not two." True emptiness and wonderful existence, however, are still within the realm of that which has marks. You must find that which is markless. The Vajra Sutra says, "All that which has marks is empty and false." That which can be spoken is false. The Sixth Patriarch said, "What has been spoken to you is not secret. If you turn the illumination inward, the secret is within you." What I am telling you now is not secret. It is the principle of the manifest teaching. You must find the secret within yourselves.

Sutra: T. 33a20

Then, Shakyamuni Buddha, wishing to accomodate his division body Buddhas, transformed in each of the eight directions, two hundred myriads of millions of nayutas of lands, purifying them all. They were without hells, hungry ghosts, animals or asuras. The gods and humans were all moved to other lands. The lands he transformed all had lapis lazuli for soil and were adorned with jeweled trees five hundred yojanas tall, decorated with branches, leaves, flowers and fruits. Beneath each tree was a jeweled lion throne, five yojanas tall decorated with various gems. There were no oceans, rivers or streams and no mucilinda or mahamucilinda mountains, no iron ring or great iron ring mountains, and no Mount Sumerus or any other kings of mountains. All became one Buddha land. The jeweled earth was level and flat, covered entirely with gem-studded canopies and hung with banners. Precious incense was burned and heavenly, precious flowers covered the ground.

Outline:

> H2. Transforming 200 myriads of millions of nayutas of lands in each of the eight directions.

Commentary:

Of the three purifications of the worlds, this is the second, the purification of worlds in each of the eight directions. Shakyamuni Buddha transformed the three thousand great thousand worlds so that the ground was made of lapis lazuli, and the roads were bordered with golden cords. He invited the Buddhas which were transformations of himself in the eastern direction to come to his Bodhimanda. However, there was not nearly enough room for them all. Seeing this, THEN SHAKYAMUNI BUDDHA, WISHING TO ACCOMODATE HIS DIVISION BODY BUDDHAS, bodies from the other directions as well as the east, TRANSFORMED IN EACH OF THE EIGHT DIRECTIONS, TWO HUNDRED MYRIADS OF MILLIONS OF NAYUTAS OF LANDS, PURIFYING THEM ALL. He used the power of his spiritual penetrations to make these lands pure. THEY WERE WITHOUT HELLS. There are many types of hells. In general, they are where offenders are punished. HUNGRY GHOSTS have stomachs as big as bass drums and throats the size of needles. Consequently, they are starving all the time but can never get enough food down to satisfy themselves. They pass through several great aeons without getting so much as a drop of water to drink. ANIMALS are horses, cows, sheep, chickens, pigs, dogs, etc. The hells, the realm of the hungry ghosts, and the animal realm are called the Three Evil Paths. Beings fall into the Three Evil Paths because of greed, hatred, and stupidity.

ASURAS are fighters. In the lands that Shakyamuni Buddha transformed, the Three Evil Paths did not exist. THE GODS AND HUMANS WERE ALL MOVED TO OTHER LANDS. They were all relocated in other worlds. THE LANDS HE TRANS- FORMED ALL HAD LAPIS LAZULI FOR SOIL AND WERE ADORNED WITH JEWELED TREES FIVE HUNDRED YOJANAS TALL, DECORATED WITH BRANCHES, LEAVES, FLOWERS AND FRUITS. They were

extremely beautiful. BENEATH EACH TREE WAS A JEWELED
LION THRONE, FIVE YOJANAS TALL DECORATED WITH VARIOUS
GEMS. THERE WERE NO OCEANS, RIVERS, OR STREAMS, AND NO
MUCILINDA OR MAHAMUCILINDA MOUNTAINS. Mucilinda is a
Sanskrit word which is interpreted as meaning, "rock
mountain." Mahamucilinda mountains are large rock mountains. Nothing grows on these bare rock mountains. NO
IRON RING OR GREAT IRON RING MOUNTAINS. The iron ring
mountains are outside of Mount Sumeru. Great iron ring
mountains are closer to, but still outside of, Mount Sumeru. "Sumeru" is also Sanskrit and means "wonderfully
high." The Four Heavenly Kings live halfway up Mount
Sumeru. OR ANY OTHER KINGS OF MOUNTAINS. Sumeru is considered the King of mountains. The Buddha has transformed these lands so that all the mountains disappear!
The land is level and flat. ALL BECAME ONE BUDDHA LAND,
the land in which Shakyamuni Buddha teaches and transforms living beings. THE JEWELED EARTH WAS LEVEL AND
FLAT. The ground was made of lapis lazuli and was very
flat. COVERED ENTIRELY WITH GEM-STUDDED CANOPIES AND
HUNG WITH BANNERS. PRECIOUS INCENSE WAS BURNED, the most
expensive kind of incense. AND HEAVENLY, PRECIOUS FLOW-
ERS COVERED THE GROUND. The ground was covered with
Mandarava flowers and other heavenly flowers.

Each one of the transformation bodies of Shakyamuni
Buddha sat in full lotus under the lion throne waiting
to see the Thus Come One Many Jewels.

Last night I explained a little bit about sitting in full lotus and the merit and virtue it brings. If those who cultivate the Way can sit in full lotus, they can give rise to the power of precepts, the power of samadhi, and the power of wisdom. If you can sit in full lotus, all the vajra Dharma protectors will protect you, all the demons will stay away from you, and all the hungry ghosts will bow to you!

In China when someone dies, monks are invited to the funeral to recite Sutras. Such monks are considered "commercial," as this is how they make their living. One time, a monk finished his recitations and was heading home at about midnight. He passed through a small village, by a house, and a dog started barking wildly. In the house, the wife said, "Take a look and see if it's a prowler." Her husband looked out the window and said, "Oh, it's just that commercial ghost!" As the monk continued on his way, it started to rain. He hid under a bridge to avoid the rain, sitting down in full lotus to meditate. Just then two ghosts came along. They were really ugly, too! Most people are scared when they see ghosts, but the monk was meditating and besides ghosts were his business, so he wasn't afraid. The two ghosts bowed to him, saying, "It's a golden pagoda. We should bow to it!" Pagodas generally contain the relics of the Buddha and when ghosts see them they always bow. Pretty soon, though, the monks's legs started to hurt and he rearranged them into half-lotus. This caused the ghosts to exclaim, "The gold pagoda has turned into silver!" Still, silver pagodas have the Buddha's relics in them, and so they continued to bow. After about half an hour, the monk's legs started hurting again and so he just stretched them out. The ghosts said, "It's not gold or silver! it's mud! Let's knock it over!!" Hearing this, he immediately pulled up into full lotus again. "Oh no! This is really inconceivable. It's a gold pagoda again. Let's bow, quick!"

The monk thought, "In full lotus, I'm a gold pagoda. In half lotus, I'm a silver pagoda. Just sitting, I'm a lump of mud." He then brought forth the Bodhi mind and resolved never to recite Sutras for money again. From then on he just meditated in full lotus every day. Sure enough, he got enlightened. "I got enlightened because those ghosts helped me out. If I hadn't met them I wouldn't be enlightened now." And he gave himself the name, "Ghost-pressured Dhyana Master."

In La Lin, in the village of Pei Yin Ho, lived Kuan Chung Hsi and his nephew Kuan Chan Hai. Kuan Chung Hsi had been a non-Buddhist teacher, and transmitted a dharma called "The Way of Gathering Conditions." He told his disciples that he had hundreds of treasures for sale at only $1,000.00 each. The treasures existed in name only, and Kuan Chung Hsi said, "The time is not right and so I can't give them to you now. When the time comes, the

world will change and you will have your treasures." He
had over four thousand disciples.

When he reached fifty years of age, he realized that
in spite of his wealth, he had nothing "precious" with
which to protect his own life. Knowing that he was close
to death and afraid to die without first understanding how
to cultivate the Way, he went with his nephew to search
for a Good Knowing Advisor, one with the five eyes and
the six spiritual penetrations, who could teach him the
fundamentals of dhyana meditation. For three years they
wandered together, visiting famous Dharma Masters in well-
known monasteries and great scholars in the academies.
They sought out hermits in lonely mountain caves, but
found no one who could teach them dhyana. Sad and disap-
pointed, they returned.

One day, I went down the mountain to buy some oil,
incense, and candles. On the way to town, I stopped to
rest at Kuan Chung Hsi's house. When the nephew saw
me, he was astonished. Pulling his uncle aside he
asked, "Who is that monk? Last night I dreamed that he
came here and sat on the brick bed. I knelt before him
and begged him to teach us the Way. In the dream he
said, 'You have a pig skin on your body which must come
off before you can cultivate," and he peeled a layer of
skin off my body and threw it on the ground. It was a
pig skin. 'You aren't a vegetarian,' the Master said,
'and you eat pork. In the future you will have a pig

skin on your back.' I was scared stiff and said to him,
'Oh no! Pigs are filthy and useless!' I had the dream
last night and now the monk is actually here. Is it a
lucky sign or not?"

His uncle was excited. "Really?" he said, "did you
really have that dream? Of course it's a lucky sign.
The monk is the Venerable Master Tu Lun, Filial Son Pai.
I've wished to bow to him for a long time and now he's
come here. It is true, then, that he has the Way and
he's brought it to our house."

After talking they went into the room where I was
sitting, closed the door, and bowed.

"Have you both gone insane?" I said. "What do you
want from me? I'm just the same as you. I don't understand the Way."

"We know you cultivate filial piety," said the uncle, "and that you have come to show us the Way. Last
night my nephew dreamed you peeled a pig skin off his
body."

"You're confused," I said. "He's not a pig. How
could I peel a pig skin off him? I can't teach you to
cultivate, but if you want to find a teacher, I can help
you look."

"We've looked everywhere," they said, "but we have
not found one. Wherever we go it's always the same. They
all have a lot of name and fame, but no genuine skill."

During the next two years, I sent them everywhere

to meet all kinds of cultivators and good knowing advisors. They continually insisted on taking me as their teacher, but I was still a young novice and didn't want any disciples. Finally, they knelt before me and refused to get up. "It's useless to talk about whether or not I I have the Way," I said. "First learn to sit in full lotus and then I will teach you."

They practiced sitting every day. The nephew had no trouble, but the uncle's bones were old and, in northeast China the mountain people have big kneecaps which stick up about fifteen inches in the air when they try to sit cross-legged. But the uncle kept trying. He pushed his knees down over and over, and in seventy days he finally managed to sit in full lotus. When I returned I noticed that the uncle's legs were swollen. They were so sore, in fact, that he couldn't even step over a cart rut. "You shouldn't sit in full lotus," I told him. "Are you still practicing?"

"I am," said the uncle.

"You shouldn't continue," I told him.

"What do you mean?" said the uncle. "I'm about to die and if I don't practice now, what will I do then? No matter what, I'm going to practice meditation. If I die, that's another matter, but as long as I'm still alive, I'm going to practice."

"Do what you like," I said, and left. When I returned a hundred days later, I noticed that the uncle's legs were no longer swollen. "You're not still sitting, are you?" I asked.

Kuan Chung Hsi smiled. "I can sit in full lotus now," he said, "and no matter how long I sit, it doesn't hurt, and my legs don't swell."

"Now I'll teach you how to work," and I instructed them saying, "Why don't living beings attain the Way? It is because of the false mind which disturbs the true nature and binds them to their passions. Defiled by greed, frustration, and discursive thought, they get caught in the flow of birth and death; they sink into the sea of suffering and lose the Way. But although the sea of suffering is boundless, a turn of the head is the other shore. Always be alert and watchful in meditation, like a chicken watching its eggs, or a dragon guarding its pearl. By and by you will get good news."

The uncle was incredibly happy and sat in meditation every day. When his death approached, he gathered his family together and said, "On such and such a day, at such and such a time, I'm going to leave; I'm going to die. The only thing I still desire is to see my teacher once again. But I don't know where he is now, and so I cannot see him." Then on the appointed day, he sat upright in full lotus, and, without any illness, he died. That evening, many of the villagers had the same dream; they dreamed that they saw the uncle accompanied by two youths in dark robes, being taken to the West.

Later, the nephew insisted on formally taking me
as his teacher. He followed me down the road until we
entered a clearing. Then suddenly he knelt, clutched
my sleeve, and begged to become a disciple. I brushed
him off and left, while the boy pleaded saying he would
not get up unless he was allowed to become a disciple.
After I had walked on a while, I turned around and saw
the boy still kneeling. I returned and accepted him as
a disciple. The boy was truly filial and always re-
spected his teacher, and although his family wasn't rich,
every New Year's he gave me a gift.

Sutra: T, 33b2

Shakyamuni Buddha, in order that the Buddhas
who were coming might have a place to sit, then
further transformed in each of the eight directions,
two hundred myriads of nayutas of lands, purifying them all. They were without hells, hungry
ghosts, animals or asuras. The gods and humans
were all moved to other lands. The lands he transformed all had lapis lazuli for soil and were
adorned with jeweled trees five hundred yojanas
tall, decorated with branches, leaves, flowers,
and fruits. Beneath each tree was a jeweled
lion throne five yojanas tall decorated with
various gems. There were no oceans, rivers, or

streams, and no mucilinda or mahamucilinda mountains, no iron ring or great iron ring mountains, and no mount sumerus or any other kings of mountains. All became one Buddha land. The jeweled earth was level and flat, covered entirely with gem-studded canopies, and hung with banners. Precious incense was burned and heavenly, precious flowers covered the ground.

Then, the division bodies of Shakyamuni Buddha from the eastern direction, Buddhas in number to the grains of sand in a hundred thousand myriads of millions of nayutas of lands, each speaking the Dharma, assembled there. In like manner, in turn, the Buddhas from all the ten directions arrived and assembled there, taking their seats in the eight directions.

At that time, each direction was filled with Buddhas, Thus Come Ones, from the four hundred myriads of millions of nayutas of lands in each of the four directions.

Outline:

> H3. Transforming 200 myriads
> of millions of nayutas of
> lands in each of the eight
> directions.

Commentary:

SHAKYAMUNI BUDDHA had too many division bodies!
There was no room for them all to sit, and so he "transformed the lands three times." Here, in the Buddhist
Lecture Hall, we have run out of room, too, and so we
are going to transform a big lecture hall!

IN ORDER THAT THE BUDDHAS WHO WERE COMING MIGHT
HAVE A PLACE TO SIT, THEN FURTHER TRANSFORMED IN EACH OF
THE EIGHT DIRECTIONS, TWO HUNDRED MYRIADS OF NAYUTAS OF
LANDS, PURIFYING THEM ALL. THEY WERE WITHOUT HELLS, HUN-
GRY GHOSTS, ANIMALS OR ASURAS. THE GODS AND HUMANS WERE
ALL MOVED TO OTHER LANDS. The gods were all moved from
this purified place into another, less clean location
for the time being. THE LANDS HE TRANSFORMED ALL HAD
LAPIS LAZULI FOR SOIL AND WERE ADORNED WITH JEWELED TREES
FIVE HUNDRED YOJANAS TALL, DECORATED WITH BRANCHES, just
like in the previous passage of text, LEAVES, FLOWERS,
AND FRUITS. BENEATH EACH TREE WAS A JEWELED LION THRONE
FIVE YOJANAS TALL DECORATED WITH VARIOUS GEMS. THERE
WERE NO OCEANS, RIVERS, OR STREAMS, AND NO MUCILINDA OR
MAHAMUCILINDA MOUNTAINS, NO IRON RING OR GREAT IRON RING
MOUNTAINS, AND NO MOUNT SUMERUS OR ANY OTHER KINGS OF

MOUNTAINS. ALL BECAME ONE BUDDHA LAND. All the two hun-
dred myriads of millions of lands in each direction be-
came one single land. THE JEWELED EARTH WAS LEVEL AND
FLAT, without mountains or valleys, COVERED ENTIRELY WITH
GEM-STUDDED CANOPIES, AND HUNG WITH BANNERS. PRECIOUS
INCENSE WAS BURNED AND HEAVENLY, PRECIOUS FLOWERS COV-
ERED THE GROUND, much nicer than carpets! Everything

was "jeweled" and "precious."

THEN, THE DIVISION BODIES OF SHAKYAMUNI BUDDHA FROM
THE EASTERN DIRECTION, BUDDHAS IN NUMBER TO THE GRAINS
OF SAND IN A HUNDRED THOUSAND MYRIADS OF MILLIONS OF NA-
YUTAS OF LANDS, EACH SPEAKING THE DHARMA, ASSEMBLED
THERE. They were in the midst of speaking the Dharma
when they gathered in Shakyamuni Buddha's assembly.
Many Jewels Thus Come One had come, on the basis of
vows he formerly made, to certify Shakyamuni Buddha's
speaking of The Dharma Flower Sutra. In order for him
to manifest in the assembly, however, he insisted that
Shakyamuni Buddha's division bodies come to the Dharma
Assembly as well.

IN LIKE MANNER, IN TURN, THE BUDDHAS FROM ALL THE
TEN DIRECTIONS... It started in the east, then went to
the south, west, north, the intermediate directions,
and up and down. They all ARRIVED AND ASSEMBLED THERE,
where Shakyamuni Buddha and Many Jewels Buddha were,
TAKING THEIR SEATS IN THE EIGHT DIRECTIONS, on all sides
of the two Buddhas.

AT THAT TIME, EACH DIRECTION WAS FILLED WITH BUD-
DHAS, THUS COME ONES FROM THE FOUR HUNDRED MYRIADS OF
MILLIONS OF NAYUTAS OF LANDS IN EACH OF THE FOUR DIREC-
TIONS. So the place was filled with the division bod-
ies of Shakyamuni Buddha!

In this Sutra, Shakyamuni Buddha transforms the
lands three times, purifying them each time. Ultimately,
what does this mean? Is this like, when we ask guests
to visit us, we first clean the house and straighten
things up out of respect for our guests? That's not the
whole story. Then what does it mean?

The first transformation represents the severing
of the delusions of views and thought.

What are the delusions of views and thought? Those
who have heard lectures on the Sutras will know, but
newer students won't be familiar with these terms. Some
will hear this explanation and understand the concepts
immediately. On the one hand, this means that they have
wisdom. On the other hand, it might mean that they listened to Sutras in former lifetimes, and so in this life
they understand them immediately.

View delusions refers to "giving rise to greed when
faced with a state." If you have cut off view delusions,
then no matter what happens, you will be "thus, thus un-
moving," and you won't be influenced by it.

You might say, "Well, I have no view delusions!"

I don't believe it! Why not? Let me ask you, if

you see someone eating something good, do you feel like eating some, too?

"No," you say.

Hah! You're probably lying. It's for sure that if people see other people eating good things, they want some, too. Those who like to drink wine will get thirsty for some if they see someone else taking a drink! That's view delusion! In general, if you see wealth, you think, "I'd like to have some more money!" and greed and delusion arise. The same applies when you see form, fame, food, or sleep. "Wouldn't a nap be nice right now?" View delusion!

Thought delusion refers to "giving rise to discrimination when confused about principle." This means that something is correct but you think, "The Dharma Master is just speaking expediently. It's not really that way, is it?" It is, but they think it isn't because they don't understand the principle in the first place. Their judgments are way off. "The Dharma Master just keeps saying the same old thing over and over. There's nothing the slightest bit true about it." In reality, every sentence is true, but because their thinking is unclear, they deny it and say it's all false. View delusion refers to confusion regarding things that are perceived. Thought delusion refers to confusion arising out of unclear thinking. The first transformation of the lands, then, refers to the severing of the delusions of views and

1734

thought.

The second transformation of the lands, purifying
them, represents the severing of delusions like dust
and sand. The delusions of views and thought are called
"coarse delusions," because they are easy to spot and
recognize. The delusions like dust and sand are much
more subtle. Such delusions are as fine as dust and as
many as grains of sand. The delusions of views and
thought are precipitated by the delusions of dust and
sand, in fact. Let's make an analogy. Your room may
appear very neat and tidy to you most of the time, without a mote of dust in it. But when the sun shines into
your room, you can see millions of millions of dust
motes bobbing around in the air, up and down! They are
only visible in the bright rays of the sun. The rays
of the sun are like your inherent wisdom. With wisdom,
you can see that you have so many delusions like dust
and sand. The delusions of dust and sand are what cause
you to give rise to so much false thinking. It seems
to come out of nowhere, all of a sudden. These delusions are very, very subtle. Stupid people have no idea
that they have false thinking all day long. They do
nothing but indulge in false thinking, and they still
think they are doing okay. They may false think about
New York, about the skyscrapers and the stock exchange.
False thinking here and there, they think themselves very
clever. Without buying a bus, plane, or train ticket, or

driving a car, they can go all the way to New York! They
think it's wonderful, but they don't realize it's just
false thinking, delusions like dust and sand. They run
around north, east, south, west, up and down, and don't
need to spend a cent! In reality, why are you getting
old? It's just because you indulge in false thinking! If
you didn't indulge in false thinking, you would always
be young. Because you have so much false thinking, you
use up all the "gasoline" in your mind, the fuel of your
life. You use it all up false thinking. Now that I have
told you this, you should understand it. False thinking
is the worst thing of all!!

The second transformation of the lands represents
severing the delusions like dust and sand.

The third transformation of lands represents severing the delusions of ignorance. When you break through
ignorance, you see the Dharma nature. I have explained
ignorance before. It is the smallest, finest kind of
delusion. It's the littlest one! It is that thing which
you just can't understand. You don't understand the Buddhadharma, that's ignorance. You don't understand why
you were born, that's ignorance. You don't understand
how you will die, that's ignorance. Whatever you don't
understand, whatever you are confused about, that's ignorance, delusion. Bodhisattvas at the level of Equal
Enlightenment still have one portion of "production mark"
ignorance which they have not broken through. If they

break through this one portion, they realize Buddhahood, and certify to the Buddha fruit. Since they haven't broken through it, they are called "Equal Enlightenment Bodhisattvas."

How many portions of ignorance do we have remaining? Limitless and boundless amounts of ignorance! We haven't broken through the delusions like dust and sand and the delusions of ignorance keep piling up behind them. The delusions like dust and sand arise with the aid of the delusions of ignorance. What helps ignorance arise? Stupidity helps ignorance arise.

Therefore, in The Dharma Flower Sutra, Shakyamuni Buddha transforms the lands three times. The meaning behind this is to cause us to cut off the three delusions: 1) the delusions of views and thought, 2) the delusions like dust and sand, and 3) the delusions of ignorance.

The three transformations of the lands has yet another interpretation. It represents the power of the Eight Liberations, the Eight Victorious Places, and the Ten All-places. The power of these three sets of Dharmas enables us to turn away from confusion and go towards enlightenment.

The Eight Liberations, also called the Eight Castings Off the Back, are:

1. The liberation in which inwardly there is the mark of   form   and outwardly   form   is contemplated.

2. The liberation in which inwardly there is no

mark of   form and outwardly   form   is contemplated.

4. The liberation in which the pure body of wisdom certifies to the complete dwelling.

4. The liberation of the station of boundless emptiness.

5. The liberation of the station of boundless consciousness.

6. The liberation of the station of nothing whatsoever.

7. The liberation of the station of neither perception nor non-perception.

8. The liberation of the samadhi of the extinction of the skandhas of feeling and thought.

The Eight Victorious Places are:

1. The victorious place in which inwardly there is the thought of form and outwardly a small amount of form is contemplated.

2. The victorious place in which inwardly there is the thought of form and outwardly a large amount of form is contemplated.

3. The victorious place in which inwardly there is no thought of form and outwardly a small amount of form is contemplated.

4. The victorious place in which inwardly there is no thought of form and outwardly a large amount of form is contemplated.

5. The victorious place of green.

6. The victorious place of yellow.

7. The victorious place of red.

8. The victorious place of white.

The Ten All-places refer to the contemplation of: green, yellow, red, white, earth, air, fire, water, consciousness, and emptiness.

The Eight Liberations, Eight Victorious Places and Ten All-places are called the three samadhis. They are three types of contemplations used in practicing Dhyana.

The Eight Liberations are also called Eight Castings Off the Back because, by means of this contemplation, one turns one's back on the states associated with the six sense objects and the five desires.

The Eight Victorious Places refer to the attainment of victorious knowledge and victorious views. Victorious knowledge means that your knowledge is correct. Victorious views means that your views are correct and you would not be upside down.

Those who cultivate Dhyana meditation must understand these states and then they can "break through the original investigation." That means they can get enlightened. They break through their "hua-t'ou." The Venerable Master Hsü-lao said,

> The home is broken up,
>
> the people are gone;
>
> It's hard to speak about it.

Empty space has also broken apart. There is no more empty

space. This is describing such a state as one attains when one "breaks through the original investigation."

The three transformations of the land apply to these Dhyana meditation techniques. The first transformation refers to the Eight Liberations. The second transformation refers to the Eight Victorious Places. The third transformation refers to the Ten All-places.

So it's not enough just to recite the words of the Sutras! You must understand their inner meanings to enter into the Sutra Store and gain wisdom like the sea. As long as you simply recite them without understanding the principles, you remain on the outside, and can't enter into them. Thus, you can't gain wisdom like the sea and you remain caught up in afflictions and united to ignorance. You "eat" afflictions, "sleep" with ignorance and "meditate" with the coarse delusions, fine delusions, and the delusions like dust and sand. If you understand the Sutras, then you can leave them behind. Otherwise, you'll be confused by them.

Sutra : T. 33 b 16

At that time, all those Buddhas each seated on a lion throne beneath a jeweled tree, sent an attendant to inquire after Shakyamuni Buddha giving them each a sack full of flowers and saying to them, "Good men! Go to Mount Grdhrakuta, to the place of Shakyamuni Buddha and ask, in our name, 'Are you free from illness and distress? Are you strong and at ease? Are the hosts of Bodhisattvas and Sound hearers at peace?' Then scatter these precious flowers before the Buddha as an offering, saying, 'The Buddha so-and-so wishes that the jeweled stupa be opened.'" All the Buddhas sent attendants in this manner.

Outline:

> G7. All the Buddhas wish
> that the stupa be opened.
> H1. The Buddhas all
> make inquiries and
> state their wishes.

Commentary:

AT THAT TIME, right after Shakyamuni Buddha had transformed the lands three times, ALL THOSE BUDDHAS, all the division bodies of Shakyamuni Buddha, EACH SEATED ON A LION THRONE BENEATH A JEWELED TREE, SENT

AN ATTENDANT, a Bodhisattva from his own Buddhaland. Before it said that each Buddha brought a Bodhisattva with him as an attendant. Now, each Buddha sent his attendant TO INQUIRE AFTER SHAKYAMUNI BUDDHA, to go there and inquire after his well-being, GIVING THEM EACH

A SACK FULL OF FLOWERS AND SAYING TO THEM, "GOOD MEN!
GO TO MOUNT GRDHRAKUTA, to Magic Mountain, Vulture Peak,
the Bodhimanda of Shakyamuni Buddha, AND ASK IN OUR NAME
'ARE YOU FREE FROM ILLNESS AND DISTRESS? You don't have
any afflictions, do you? ARE YOU STRONG AND AT EASE?
You aren't over-taxing yourself, are you? ARE THE HOSTS
OF BODHISATTVAS AND SOUND HEARERS AT PEACE?'

Sound Hearers are those who awoke to the Way upon
hearing Shakyamuni Buddha speak the Dharma. There are
also the Conditioned Enlightened Ones who cultivated
the Twelve Causal Links. The Sound Hearers cultivate
the Four Truths. What are the Four Truths? Suffering,
origination, extinction, and the Way.

We have already discussed the Three Sufferings, the
Eight Sufferings, and all the limitless sufferings. Origination refers to afflictions. Extinction refers to
the extinction of afflictions. The Way is the path to
the extinction.

The Twelve Causal Conditions cultivated by the Conditioned Enlightened Ones are:

1) ignorance, which conditions

2) activity, which conditions

3) consciousness, which conditions

4) name and form, which conditions

5) the six sense organs, which conditions

6) contact, which conditions

7) feeling, which conditions

8) craving, which conditions

9) grasping, which conditions

10) becoming, which conditions

11) birth, which conditions

12) old age and death.

When born during the time when a Buddha is in the world, they are called Conditioned Enlightened Ones, because they contemplate the Twelve Causal Conditions and thereby become enlightened. When born at a time when there is no Buddha in the world, they are called Solitarily Enlightened Ones. They live deep in the mountains by themselves. In the spring they watch the white flowers bloom, and in the fall they watch the yellow leaves fall. They see that the ten thousand things are born and then die over and over, from emptiness to existence and from existence to emptiness, and in this way they get enlightened.

Here in the text, the term Sound Hearers refers to Sound Hearers and Conditioned Enlightened Ones. "Are the hosts of Bodhisattvas and Sound Hearers at peace? Is everybody happy? There haven't been any problems, have there?"

"THEN SCATTER THESE PRECIOUS FLOWERS BEFORE THE BUDDHA AS AN OFFERING, SAYING, 'THE BUDDHA SO-AND-SO WISHES THAT THE JEWELED STUPA BE OPENED. We all want the Stupa opened so we can see the Buddha Many Jewels.'" ALL THE BUDDHAS SENT ATTENDANTS IN THIS MANNER. All the division bodies of Shakyamuni Buddha in the three

thousand great thousand worlds, each of two hundred
myriads of millions of nayutas of lands--that's counting the second transformation of the land. If you count
the third transformation, which was also two hundred
myriads of millions of nayutas of lands, that makes four
hundred myriads of millions of nayutas of lands. Multi-
ply that by the eight directions and you get thirty-two
hundred myriads of millions of nayutas of lands!

Sutra : T. 33b23

Then, Shakyamuni Buddha, seeing that the
division body Buddhas had all assembled there,
each seated on a lion throne, and hearing that
all the Buddhas together wished that the jeweled
stupa be opened, immediately arose from his seat
into empty space. All those in the four assemblies rose, placed their palms together, and
singlemindedly beheld the Buddha.

Then, Shakyamuni Buddha, using his right-
forefinger, opened the door of the stupa of seven
jewels, which made a great sound like that of a
bolt being removed from a large city gate.

Outline:

H2. Shakyamuni Buddha
opens the Stupa.

Commentary:

All the Buddhas which were transformations of Shakyamuni Buddha sent their attendants to inquire after
Shakyamuni Buddha. THEN, SHAKYAMUNI BUDDHA, SEEING THAT
THE DIVISION BODY BUDDHAS HAD ALL ASSEMBLED THERE...
When Shakyamuni Buddha used the power of his spiritual
penetrations to observe the situation, he saw that all
the division body Buddhas had, in fact, arrived.

EACH SEATED ON A LION THRONE.   Each of the division
body Buddhas were sitting on a Lion Throne beneath a
Bodhi Tree.   AND HEARING THAT ALL THE BUDDHAS TOGETHER,
all the division bodies, WISHED THAT THE JEWELED STUPA
BE OPENED, IMMEDIATELY AROSE FROM HIS SEAT INTO EMPTY
SPACE.   He got up and rose up into empty space.

ALL THOSE IN THE FOUR ASSEMBLIES, Bhikshus, Bhikshunis, Upasakas, Upasikas, ROSE, PLACED THEIR PALMS
TOGETHER, AND SINGLEMINDEDLY BEHELD THE BUDDHA.   Everyone stood up to get a good view of Shakyamuni Buddha
opening the jeweled Stupa.

THEN, SHAKYAMUNI BUDDHA, USING HIS RIGHT FOREFIN-
GER, OPENED THE DOOR OF THE STUPA OF SEVEN JEWELS,
WHICH MADE A GREAT SOUND LIKE THAT OF A BOLT BEING RE-
MOVED FROM A LARGE CITY GATE.

"Using his right forefinger" represents the use of
the provisional teaching.   "To open the Stupa" represents the "opening of the provisional."   "Seeing the
Buddha" represents the manifesting of the actual teach-

ing. This means that the former provisional teaching,
the expedient teaching, is dispensed with so that the
real actual Dharma-door can manifest.

Sutra: T. 33b28

Thereupon, the entire assembly perceived the
Thus Come One Many Jewels seated upon the lion
throne inside the jeweled stupa, his body whole
and undecayed as if he were in dhyana samadhi. They also heard him say, "Good indeed!
Good indeed! Shakyamuni Buddha! Quickly
speak The Dharma Flower Sutra! I came here
to hear this sutra!"

The four assemblies, upon seeing a Buddha
who had crossed over into extinction limitless
thousands of myriads of millions of aeons ago,
speak in this way, praised it as something unprecedented, they scattered heaps of precious
heavenly flowers upon the Buddha Many
Jewels and Shakyamuni Buddha.

Outline:

H3. What the four as-
semblies see and hear.

Commentary:

THEREUPON, right after Shakyamuni Buddha opened the

door of the jeweled Stupa, THE ENTIRE ASSEMBLY PERCEIVED
THE THUS COME ONE MANY JEWELS SEATED UPON THE LION
THRONE ISNIDE THE JEWELED STUPA, HIS BODY WHOLE AND
UNDECAYED; it was in perfect condition. AS IF HE WERE
IN DHYANA SAMADHI, meditating. THEY ALSO HEARD HIM SAY,
"GOOD INDEED! GOOD INDEED! SHAKYAMUNI BUDDHA! This is
just great! I have come here to certify this Dharma As-
sembly. I ask that you QUICKLY SPEAK THE DHARMA FLOWER
SUTRA! Hurry up and speak it. I CAME HERE TO HEAR
THIS SUTRA! That's why I am here!"

THE FOUR ASSEMBLIES, UPON SEEING A BUDDHA WHO HAD
CROSSED OVER INTO EXTINCTION LIMITLESS THOUSANDS OF
MYRIADS OF MILLIONS OF AEONS AGO, SPEAK IN THIS WAY...
He had entered Nirvana so very long ago and yet now
he had come to this Dharma assembly to praise Shakya-
muni Buddha and ask him to hurry and speak The Dharma
Flower Sutra. Everyone PRAISED IT AS SOMETHING UNPRE-
CEDENTED. They were all really surprised! They had
never seen such a thing before. THEY SCATTERED HEAPS
OF PRECIOUS HEAVENLY FLOWERS UPON THE BUDDHA MANY JEW-
ELS AND SHAKYAMUNI BUDDHA, as tokens of their reverence.

Sutra : T. 33 c 5
    The Buddha Many Jewels, in the jeweled
stupa, offered half of his seat to Shakyamuni
Buddha, saying, "Shakyamuni Buddha, would
you take this seat?" Shakyamuni Buddha then

entered the stupa and sat down in full lotus on half of that seat.

Outline: H4. The two Buddhas
                              share the seat.

Commentary:

THE BUDDHA MANY JEWELS, IN THE JEWELED STUPA, OF-
FERED HALF OF HIS SEAT TO SHAKYAMUNI BUDDHA, SAYING,
"SHAKYAMUNI BUDDHA, WOULD YOU TAKE THIS SEAT?   There's
room for one more here. We can share." SHAKYAMUNI
BUDDHA THEN ENTERED THE STUPA without further ado, say-
ing, "Okay, I'll take half," AND SAT DOWN IN FULL LOTUS
ON HALF OF THAT SEAT. He didn't sit casually; he sat
upright in full lotus.

Sutra T. 33 c 8

The great assembly, seeing the two Thus Come Ones seated in the jeweled stupa in full lotus on the lion throne, all had this thought, "The Buddhas are sitting up so high and far off. We only wish that the Thus Come One would use the power of his spiritual penetrations and enable us all to dwell in empty space."

Shakyamuni Buddha then used his spiritual powers and took the entire assembly up into empty space."

Outline:

> H5. The four assem-
> blies ask to be taken
> into empty space.

Commentary;

THE GREAT ASSEMBLY, SEEING THE TWO THUS COME ONES SEATED IN THE JEWELED STUPA IN FULL LOTUS, ON THE LION THRONE, ALL HAD THIS THOUGHT, "They are really good buddies! THE BUDDHAS ARE SITTING UP SO HIGH AND FAR OFF. We can hardly see them. They may be speaking loudly, but still they are so far away. WE ONLY WISH THAT THE THUS COME ONE WOULD USE THE POWER OF HIS SPIR- ITUAL PENETRATIONS AND ENABLE US ALL TO DWELL IN EMPTY SPACE. We all want to go up into empty space. Wouldn't that be great?" That's what they were all thinking.

SHAKYAMUNI BUDDHA THEN, because he had the power to read the others' minds, saw that these kiddies were just having false thinking and that if he didn't take them up there too, they might start crying! So he USED HIS SPIRITUAL POWERS AND TOOK THE ENTIRE ASSEMBLY UP INTO EMPTY SPACE. They stood right there in empty space!

Sutra: T. 33c 12

With a great voice he addressed the four assemblies, saying: Who, in this saha land, can broadly speak this sutra of the Dharma Flower? Now is the proper time, for the Thus Come One will shortly enter Nirvana. The Buddha wishes to bequeath The Dharma Flower Sutra."

Outline:

F3. Shakyamuni Buddha
announces his appeal.

Commentary:

WITH A GREAT VOICE HE ADDRESSED THE FOUR ASSEM-
BLIES, Bhikshus, Bhikshunis, Upasakas, Upasikas, SAY-
ING: WHO IN THIS SAHA LAND CAN BROADLY SPEAK THIS
SUTRA OF THE DHARMA FLOWER? This Saha World, one
filled with myriad evils..."Broadly" means to speak it
every day, like we do here at the Buddhist Lecture Hall.
Why are we doing this every day? Because at that time,
when the Buddha asked everyone, we made vows. You said,
"I want to lecture on it!" So, now when the world is
so torn with war and strife and in such a dangerous situation, we still countinue to lecture on the Sutra here
at the Buddhist Lecture Hall. This is truly a case of
"doing what is difficult to do." It's very hard. We
don't charge any money and most people aren't interested

or don't know about this Dharma Flower Assembly. If you want to study the Buddhadharma, and you don't come here to listen to the Sutra, you can't be said to be really studying it. Today, I am telling you the plain truth. We are really upholding and practicing the Buddhadharma here.

"NOW IS THE PROPER TIME for those of you who want to propagate The Dharma Flower Sutra. Come forth! Make vows! Don't wait! Don't stare at each other and hold back. Hurry and make vows to teach The Dharma Flower Sutra. FOR THE THUS COME ONE WILL SHORTLY ENTER NIRVANA. Shakyamuni Buddha says, "Not long after I speak The Dharma Flower Sutra, I am going to enter Nirvana. THE BUDDHA WISHES TO BEQUEATH, to assign, THE DHARMA FLOWER SUTRA, to transfer the responsibility to someone.

We lecture the Buddhadharma at the Buddhist Lecture Hall, but it is really too bitter here. We get up at four in the morning, start reciting and then meditate and keep on working right through the day until nine at night. It's really an impossible schedule!

The problem is, if you insist that everything be "possible" you won't be able to investigate the genuine Buddhadharma. If you want to investigate the real Dharma, you have to take what you can't take, and digest what you can't digest! Then, there's hope for you. If you retreat the moment you run into some hardship or pain, then you're useless. To the ends of time, you'll never master the real Buddhadharma. If you want to learn the genuine Buddhadharma, you must go where it is really "bitter." The Buddhist Lecture Hall keeps the same schedule for cultivation, regardless of whether or not people come.

There are quite a few people here this summer for the Summer Session, but even if there was only one person, we would still do things the same way. If ten thousand people came, we would still do things the same way. The Dharma here flows like running water, every day.

This year for Kuan Yin's anniversary we are going to set free five hundred pigeons in a Liberating Life Ceremony. Someone is thinking, "In the future they will turn into five hundred Buddhas or five hundred Arhats!" We shouldn't have this kind of false thinking. We should just go ahead and set them free. Today you all saw the two pigeons, Seven Bodhi Shares and Twelve Links? As soon as they saw me, they flew over and landed on my arms. These pigeons were in the group of thirty-four pigeons that we released a while back. They were the only two who came back. They are quite radiant and very obedient. When I told them to "come upstairs" they climbed up on my arms! They are very good!

Several people now are thinking about taking refuge. However, you must be even more obedient than these pigeons! You can't be worse than a pigeon! After this,

if I tell you to do something, you can't refuse. If
you do that, your teacher who finds "everything okay"
might find things not okay!

Sutra: T. 33c15
  The World Honored One, wishing to restate
this meaning, spoke verses saying:
  The sagely lord, World Honored One,
  Although long extinct
  Within this jeweled stupa
  Has come here for the Dharma.
  Who would not be diligent
  For the sake of the Dharma?
  This Buddha became extinct
  Countless aeons ago and yet,
  In place after place, he listens to the Dharma,
  Because it is difficult to encounter.
  In the past this Buddha made a vow,
  "After my extinction,
  I will go everywhere
  In order to hear the Dharma."

Outline:

                    E2. Verse

                       F1. Verses about Many Jewels.

Commentary:

In this section of verse, Many Jewels Thus Come One is praised for his vow. He vowed to come and listen wherever The Dharma Flower Sutra was being spoken. If the Buddha Many Jewels goes out of his way like this, how much the more so should we ordinary people make an effort to listen to it! THEN THE WORLD HONORED ONE, WISHING TO RESTATE HIS MEANING, SPOKE VERSES SAYING:

THE SAGELY LORD, WORLD HONORED ONE/ This is praising Many Jewels Thus Come One. He is honored by the title "Sagely Lord." "World Honored" means that he is the most honored both in and beyond the world.

ALTHOUGH LONG EXTINCT/ Even though limitless, limitless aeons ago he passed into extinction, went to Nirvana, WITHIN THIS JEWELED STUPA/ HAS COME HERE FOR THE DHARMA/ He came to hear the Dharma. Basically, he had already become a Buddha and didn't need to listen to the Dharma. Still, he came to listen.

WHO WOULD NOT BE DILIGENT/ FOR THE SAKE OF THE DHARMA?/ Since the Buddha is so diligent, not fearing difficulty, not being lazy, why aren't we common folk diligent in our quest for the Dharma? Why are we lazy? For example, you might know quite clearly that the Sutra is being lectured but still not come to listen. Or else one might come and listen, but refuse to believe it. Or, if one believes it, one may fail to practice.

Those who truly believe in the Buddha will always

come to lectures on the Dharma, regardless of how busy
they are. Listening to the Sutra lectures should be
regarded as more important than life itself. It is
essential to listen to the lectures.

THIS BUDDHA BECAME EXTINCT/ COUNTLESS AEONS AGO,
AND YET/ Numberless kalpas ago. IN PLACE AFTER PLACE,
HE LISTENS TO THE DHARMA/ Wherever The Dharma Flower
Sutra is being lectured, he goes to listen, especially
when the Buddha speaks it. He manifests his jeweled
Stupa in empty space to certify the speaking of the
Sutra.

Why does the Buddha Many Jewels, already a Buddha,
still come to listen to The Dharma Flower Sutra? BE-
CAUSE IT IS DIFFICULT TO ENCOUNTER/ You could say,

> Supreme, profound, wonderful Dharma
> Is hard to meet in a million aeons.
> I now see, hear, and uphold it,
> And vow to understand the Thus Come One's
> genuine meaning.

Because it is so hard to encounter, Many Jewels
Thus Come One has vowed to go and listen to it where-
ever it is being spoken.

IN THE PAST, THIS BUDDHA MADE A VOW/ Why, after all
these aeons, did he come to certify the Buddha's speaking of the Sutra? Because of a vow he made long ago.
He vowed that "AFTER MY EXTINCTION/ I WILL GO EVERYWHERE/

IN ORDER TO HEAR THE DHARMA/ The Dharma Flower Sutra is very difficult to encounter. When I become a Buddha, it's for sure that I am going to protect the Bodhimanda in which the Buddha is speaking The Dharma Flower Sutra. I will certainly go there and protect it."

Why did he make such a strange vow? To manifest his jeweled Stupa when the Sutra is being taught? It was because this Sutra is so very important. It is said that The Dharma Flower is the Sutra for becoming a Buddha. Therefore, the Buddha Many Jewels vowed that in any land where The Dharma Flower Sutra was being spoken, he would always go and listen. He wasn't like us now. We haven't even become Buddhas, and we neglect to listen to the Dharma! When do we ever expect to become Buddhas? Nobody could figure out when, because it's just way too far in the future--out of sight.

Someone is thinking, "Well, I always come to the lectures!"

Fine, but you don't listen.

Someone else is thinking, "But I listen! I listen to every word you say. But it's in Chinese and I don't understand it! The English translation is sometimes not always reliable, so I get about half."

Someone else says, "I know Chinese and English! So it's for sure I hear it. I hear it, but I don't think it's all that wonderful."

So I say, some hear it and don't believe it. Who

would have guessed this very stupid teacher would catch
these trains of thought?

Someone else says, "I believe it totally. I know
it is an inconceivable state."

So I say, you might believe it, but you don't
practice it! You don't cultivate according to it.

Another disciple objects. "I hear it and then I
practice it!"

Really? Perhaps for two and a half days. By the
time the third day rolls around, you've forgotten it entirely.

Another very sincere disciple says, "From the time
I started hearing the Dharma until now, I have put every
principle into practice, unless I forgot about it. My
memory isn't so good, so even though I might want to
practice, I sometimes forget."

Those who want to practice, forget and those who
remember don't want to practice. Ahh!! Just listening
isn't as good as practicing. And you can't just practice for a couple days and then forget all about it.
Wouldn't you say the Dharma was difficult to accept?
You can also say that living beings are just living beings, and they are extremely difficult to teach and
transform.

They are hard to teach, but I don't care. The harder they are to teach, the harder I try to teach them.
That's why I go right ahead and lecture on The Dharma

<u>Flower</u> <u>Sutra</u>. If you listen, fine. If you don't listen, I will listen to myself. "Hmm!! Listen to that. I'm lecturing on <u>The</u> <u>Dharma</u> <u>Flower</u> <u>Sutra</u>. Doing a great job, too! Wonderful!!"

See? Whether you listen or not, I don't get angry. I wouldn't say, "You better listen to my lectures, or I'm going to blast you a good one." Not me.

Sutra : T. 33c21

Also, my division bodies,
Limitless Buddhas,
Equal in number to the Ganges' sands
Have come, wishing to hear the Dharma
And to see the extinct
Thus Come One, Many Jewels.
Casting aside their wondrous lands
And assemblies of disciples
Gods, people, dragons and spirits,
And various offerings,
They have come here
To cause the Dharma long to abide.
In order to seat those Buddhas,
I have used my spiritual powers,
To move countless multitudes
And purify the lands.

1758

Each one of the Buddhas
Takes his place beneath a jeweled tree
Like a lotus adorning
A clear, clean pond.
Beneath the jeweled trees,
There are lion thrones
Upon which the Buddhas sit,
Adorned with brilliant light,
Like great torches gleaming
In the darkness of the night.
Their bodies emit a delicate fragrance
Pervading the ten direction lands
All beings perfumed by it
Are overwhelmed with joy.
Like a great wind
Blowing the small trees,
By means of this expedient device,
The Dharma is caused long to abide.

Outline:

F2. Verses about the division
bodies.

Commentary:

ALSO, MY DIVISION BODIES/ Shakyamuni Buddha continues, LIMITLESS BUDDHAS/ They are EQUAL IN NUMBER TO THE

GANGES' SANDS/ HAVE COME, WISHING TO HEAR THE DHARMA/
AND TO SEE THE EXTINCT/ THUS COME ONE, MANY JEWELS/ who
entered Nirvana long, long ago. CASTING ASIDE THEIR WON-
DROUS LANDS/ each division body casting aside his subtle,
fine, country AND ASSEMBLIES OF DISCIPLES/ Basically, the
Buddhas are especially close to their disciples. This is
because living beings are just the Buddha's heart. Therefore, the Buddhas wouldn't ever let go of living beings.
The Buddha's all cherish their disciples, like parents
cherish their children. Some of you are thinking of visiting your parents, and your parents have even offered
to pay your plane fare, round trip! This is because they
can't let you go! That's how the Buddhas feel about
their disciples. I am rather lacking in compassion towards my disciples and not very good to them, however,
I'll tell you plainly.

GODS, PEOPLE, DRAGONS, AND SPIRITS/ AND VARIOUS
OFFERINGS/ THEY HAVE COME HERE/ TO CAUSE THE DHARMA
LONG TO ABIDE/ So the Buddhadharma can dwell in the
world for a long, long time. The Stupa of the Thus Come
One Many Jewels has manifested in empty space, and all
the division body Buddhas of Shakyamuni Buddha have come
here all in order to cause the Dharma to endure in the
world for a long time. IN ORDER TO SEAT THOSE BUDDHAS/
I HAVE USED MY SPIRITUAL POWERS/ TO MOVE COUNTLESS MUL-
TITUDES/ AND PURIFY THE LANDS/ Because I wanted each
of the Buddhas to have a place to sit, I have moved all

the countless beings of the hell, animal, and hungry
ghost realms, as well as the gods and asuras, somewhere
else, to another land. In this way, the world is purified. There is no defiled energy in it.

I will give you an example. Let's say someone has
a lot of cats and dogs who aren't very sanitary in their
habits and generally stink up the place. Let's say that
an important guest is coming, so the cats are hustled
off to their houses and the dogs are taken to the kennel.
Then he cleans the room and sprays it with deodorizer,
so it's all nice and clean. The same principle applies
here in the Sutra. All the unclean beings have been
moved away for the occasion.

EACH ONE OF THE BUDDHAS/ TAKES HIS PLACE BENEATH A
JEWELED TREE/ LIKE A LOTUS ADORNING/ A CLEAR, CLEAN POND/
The Buddha purified the worlds three times, cleaning
everything up real nice, and all the division bodies were
sitting under their Bodhi trees like lotuses sitting in
a crystal clear pond.

BENEATH THE JEWELED TREES/ THERE ARE LION THRONES/
UPON WHICH THE BUDDHAS SIT/ The Bodhi trees are five hundred yojanas tall and the Lion Thrones are five yojanas
tall. ADORNED WITH BRILLIANT LIGHT/ They are a treasury
of bright light. LIKE GREAT TORCHES GLEAMING/ IN THE
DARKNESS OF THE NIGHT/ The world, which is in darkness,
is illumined by the light emitted from the Buddhas.

THEIR BODIES EMIT A DELICATE FRAGRANCE/ People who

cultivate and, life after life, keep the precepts, will always have bodies which emit the fragrance of a lotus. It won't be as strong as perfume. It's very subtle. PERVADING THE TEN DIRECTION LANDS/ ALL BEINGS PERFUMED BY IT/ ARE OVERWHELMED WITH JOY/ They are delighted! Their tempers all disappear. They don't know where all their anger ran off too! LIKE A GREAT WIND/ BLOWING ON THE SMALL TRESS/

BY MEANS OF THIS EXPEDIENT DEVICE/ THE DHARMA IS CAUSED LONG TO ABIDE/

Sutra: T. 34 a 4
To the great assembly, J say:
"After my extinction
Who can protect and uphold,
Read, speak and recite this sutra?
Now, in the presence of the Buddhas
He should make a vow.

Outline:

F3. Verses about bequeathing.
G1. Three Buddhas' (Shakyamuni, Many Jewels, and the division bodies) exhortation to propagate the Sutra.
H1. Searching for the person.

1762

Commentary:

TO THE GREAT ASSEMBLY, I SAY:/ AFTER MY EXTINCTION/
WHO CAN PROTECT AND UPHOLD/

Shakyamuni Buddha said, "I am just about done speaking The Dharma Flower Sutra and am getting ready to enter
Nirvana.   After My extinction, who can protect and uphold? Who of you in the four assemblies here can make a
vow to support this Sutra, READ, SPEAK, AND RECITE THIS
SUTRA?/ NOW, IN THE PRESENCE OF THE BUDDHAS/ Me, Shakyamuni Buddha, and Many Jewels Thus Come One, and all my
division body Buddhas, HE SHOULD MAKE A VOW/ Make
your vows now! This is like here in the Lecture Hall
some people made vows. Everyone makes their own vows.
After hearing this Sutra, some of you may make vows to
protect The Dharma Flower Sutra and support those who
are lecturing on it.

Sutra: T. 34a6
    The Buddha Many Jewels
    Although long extinct
    By means of his great vow
    Utters the lion's roar.
    The Thus Come One Many Jewels,
    As well as myself,
    And the transformation Buddhas here
        assembled

Will know of this resolution .
All you disciples of the Buddha,
Whoever can protect this Dharma ,
Should make a great vow
To cause the Dharma long to abide .

Outline:

H2. The three Buddhas exhortation to hold the Sutra.

Commentary:

THE BUDDHA MANY JEWELS/ ALTHOUGH LONG EXTINCT/ BY
MEANS OF HIS GREAT VOW/ UTTERS THE LION'S ROAR/ from
within the Great Stupa. THE THUS COME ONE MANY JEWELS/
AS WELL AS MYSELF/ Shakyamuni Buddha, AND THE TRANSFORMA-
TION BUDDHAS HERE ASSEMBLED/ who have gathered here, WILL
KNOW OF THIS RESOLUTION/ When you make your vow, we will
all know what your intentions are. ALL OF YOU DISCI-
PLES OF THE BUDDHA/ WHOEVER CAN PROTECT THIS DHARMA/
SHOULD MAKE A GREAT VOW/ TO CAUSE THE DHARMA LONG TO
ABIDE/ Make this great vow so that the Dharma of The
Dharma Flower Sutra can dwell in the world for a long
time to come.

Sutra: T. 34a 10
Whoever can protect
The Dharma of this sutra,

The Buddha Many Jewels
Has thereby made offerings
To me and Many Jewels.
Dwelling in the jeweled stupa,
Always travels throughout the ten directions,
For the sake of this sutra.
Moreover, they will have made offerings,
To the transformation Buddhas here,
Who adorn with splendor,
All the worlds.
If one speaks this sutra,
They will then see me,
The Thus Come One Many Jewels,
And the transformation Buddhas.

Outline:

> H3. Shakyamuni Buddha's ex-
>
> hortation.

Commentary:

WHOEVER CAN PROTECT/ Shakyamuni Buddha says, "I am
now just about done with The Lotus Sutra. I am then
going to enter into Nirvana, so you should all make vows
to protect, uphold and propagate The Dharma Flower Sutra,
and cause this wonderful dharma to remain in the world
for a long time. THE DHARMA OF THIS SUTRA/ HE HAS THERE-

BY MADE OFFERINGS/ TO ME AND MANY JEWELS/ Why? The Wonderful Dharma Lotus Flower Sutra is my real body. Not only have they made offerings to me, but also to the Thus Come One Many Jewels.

THE BUDDHA MANY JEWELS/ DWELLING IN THE JEWELED STUPA/ ALWAYS TRAVELS THROUGHOUT THE TEN DIRECTIONS/ FOR THE SAKE OF THIS SUTRA/ He certifies the speaking of The Dharma Flower Sutra.

MOREOVER, THEY WILL HAVE MADE OFFERINGS/ TO THE TRANSFORMATION BUDDHAS HERE/ WHO ADORN WITH SPLENDOR/ ALL OF THE WORLDS/ If you can lecture on The Dharma Flower Sutra, you are making offerings to all the transformation Buddhas who illumine the world with their light.

IF ONE SPEAKS THIS SUTRA/ THEY WILL THEN SEE ME/ Shakyamuni Buddha, THE THUS COME ONE MANY JEWELS/ AND THE TRANSFORMATION BUDDHAS/ the limitless transformation bodies.

Sutra : T. 34 a 15
All of you good men
Think it over carefully!
This is a difficult matter
Requiring a great vow.

Outline:

> > G2. The difficulty of upholding
> > the Dharma and exhortation to
> > propagate it.
> > > H1. Exhorting.
> > > > I1. Sincere exhortation.

Commentary:

ALL OF YOU GOOD MEN/ and good women, THINK IT OVER
CAREFULLY!/ THIS IS A DIFFICULT MATTER/ It is a very
difficult matter to make a vow to protect, uphold,
preach, and lecture upon The Dharma Flower Sutra. It is
not a simple matter. It is difficult even to come to
listen to it being lectured. You might want to hear lectures on it, but no one will be lecturing it. How are
you going to hear it then? You can't lecture on it yourself. It is no easy matter. What's to be done? You
should make a vow. REQUIRING A GREAT VOW. Make vows,
saying:

> In every life I will draw near to the Triple
> > Jewel.
> In every life I will protect and uphold The
> > Wonderful Dharma Lotus Flower Sutra.
> In every life I will take refuge with a Good
> > Knowing Advisor.
> In every life I will listen to my Good Knowing
> > Advisor lecture on The Dharma Flower Sutra.

If you make vows, you will have a chance to hear this
Sutra. Otherwise, when it is being lectured, you might
not want to hear it. You might get one foot in the
door, but the other foot will carry you off somewhere
else! Gone! No chance to hear the Sutra. Just to have
it together enough to come and listen to the lectures
is quite inconceivable. Didn't I teach you in Chinese
Class today the phrase from my book, Water Mirror Turning Back Heaven,

> Who would have thought the Buddhadharma
> was anything but inconceivable!

It's just describing the inconceivable state of The
Dharma Flower Sutra.

Sutra : T. 34 a 16

> Other sutras number
> Like the Ganges river's sands
> But although one spoke them,
> It would not be thought difficult.

> If one took Mount Sumeru
> And tossed it to another land
> Across countless Buddha lands,
> That also would not be difficult.

> Or if with a toe
> One kicked the great thousand worlds

To another, far-off land,
That also would not be difficult.

Were one to stand on the peak of being
And for the multitudes proclaim,
Limitless other sutras,
That, too, would not be difficult.

But if after the Buddha's extinction
Within the evil age,
One can speak this sutra,
That is difficult.

If someone took
Empty space in his hand
And wandered around with it
That would not be difficult.

But if, after my extinction
One can write out and uphold it
And encourage others to write it out,
That is difficult.

If one were to take the earth
And place it on one's toenail,
And carry it up to the Brahma heavens,
That, too, would not be difficult.

After the Buddha's extinction,
In the evil age
To read this sutra but for an instant,
That is difficult.

If, during the fire at the kalpa's end
One carried a load of dry grass on one's back
And entering the fire was not burned
That would not be difficult.

But after my extinction
If one can uphold the sutra
And speak it to a single person,
That is difficult.

If one upheld eighty four-thousand
Dharma treasuries
And the twelve divisions of the canon
Expounding upon them to others
Causing all the listeners
To gain the six spiritual penetrations,
Even if one could do this
It would not be difficult.
But if, after my extinction,
One can listen to and accept this sutra
And inquire into its meaning

That is difficult.
If one were to speak the Dharma
And cause a thousand myriads of millions
Of limitless, countless
Beings, like the Ganges' sands,
To obtain arhatship
And perfect the six spiritual penetrations,
Although it would be beneficial,
It would not be difficult.

But after my extinction,
If one can reverently uphold
Such a sutra as this,
That indeed is difficult!

Outline:

> I2. The difficulty of uphold-
> ing this Sutra.

Commentary:

OTHER SUTRAS NUMBER/ LIKE THE GANGES RIVER'S SANDS/
There are a lot of Buddhist Sutras. BUT ALTHOUGH ONE
SPOKE THEM/ IT WOULD NOT BE THOUGHT DIFFICULT/ A lot of
people could do that. IF ONE TOOK MOUNT SUMERU/ AND
TOSSED IT TO ANOTHER LAND/ ACROSS COUNTLESS BUDDHA LANDS/
THAT ALSO WOULD NOT BE DIFFICULT/ It wouldn't be that
hard, as long as you had spiritual powers.

OR IF WITH A TOE / ONE KICKED THE GREAT THOUSAND
WORLDS/ TO ANOTHER, FAR-OFF LAND/ THAT ALSO WOULD NOT
BE DIFFICULT/ That wouldn't be any big deal, really.
WERE ONE TO STAND ON THE PEAK OF BEING/ AND FOR
THE MULTITUDES PROCLAIM/ LIMITLESS OTHER SUTRAS/ THAT,
TOO, WOULD NOT BE DIFFICULT/ All the limitless Sutras.
Going up into the heavens to preach the Sutras is not
really that hard. You just need to have spiritual powers
like the Heavenly Eye and Heavenly Ear. BUT, IF AFTER
THE BUDDHA'S EXTINCTION/ WITHIN THE EVIL AGE/ ONE CAN
SPEAK THIS SUTRA/ THAT IS DIFFICULT!/ The evil world is
our world right now. We call it evil because it is a
world of five evil turbidities. First of all, there is
the turbidity of time. Then views are turbid because
as soon as we see something, we are defiled by our attachments and afflictions. Afflictions are turbid, and
everybody has afflictions. Living beings are turbid and
their lifespans are turbid. Therefore, the world right
now is an evil world. Why do we say this? If you do
something good everyone thinks you are stupid. They say,
"He's really stupid. Why does he give his money away
like that? Idiocy!!" People think that doing good things
and fostering virtue is stupid, and they scold you. In
the evil age people say black is white, and wrong is
right. If you do something good, people accuse you of
seeking recognition. They don't do anything good themselves, but when someone else does, they try to poison

them with their criticism. In this way people are dis-
couraged from doing good deeds.

IF SOMEONE TOOK/ EMPTY SPACE IN HIS HAND/ AND WAN-
DERED AROUND WITH IT/ THAT WOULD NOT BE DIFFICULT/ There
might or might not be such a person, because it's not
the easiest thing to do to take up empty space in your
hand and wander around here, there, and everywhere with
it, you know. But, let's say you took up all of empty
space in your hand, where would you have any space to
walk around in? Sounds like a contradiction! It's hard,
but not that hard, as long as you have the six spiritual
penetrations. BUT IF, AFTER MY EXTINCTION/ ONE CAN

WRITE OUT AND UPHOLD IT/--the Dharma Flower Sutra. "Uphold" means that you are able to recite it from memory.
AND ENCOURAGE OTHERS TO WRITE IT OUT/ THAT IS DIFFICULT/
Why? Because it is an inconceivable state. No one believes in it, as a rule.

IF ONE WERE TO TAKE THE EARTH/ the whole planet,
AND PLACE IT ON ONE'S TOENAIL/ AND CARRY IT UP TO THE
BRAHMA HEAVENS/ doing it with more ease than riding in
an elevator, THAT, TOO, WOULD NOT BE DIFFICULT/ It could
be done, but...

AFTER THE BUDDHA'S EXTINCTION/ IN THE EVIL AGE/ TO
READ THIS SUTRA BUT FOR AN INSTANT/ THAT IS DIFFICULT/ So
you see, it's not that easy to hear The Dharma Flower
Sutra, to read it, or to write it out! It's very, very
difficult.

IF, DURING THE FIRE AT THE KALPA'S END/ ONE CARRIED
A LOAD OF DRY GRASS ON ONE'S BACK/AND ENTERING THE FIRE
WAS NOT BURNED/ THAT WOULD NOT BE DIFFICULT/ At the end
of the kalpa, there are three disasters: water, fire,
and wind. When the disaster of fire strikes, there will
be seven suns appearing in the sky, and all the oceans
will be boiled dry. And we thought it was hot here yesterday! In a situation like this, even wet grass would
catch on fire.

BUT AFTER MY EXTINCTION/ IF ONE CAN UPHOLD THIS
SUTRA/ AND SPEAK IT TO A SINGLE PERSON/ THAT IS DIFFICULT/
Even just a single person! It's really difficult. And
here I am lecturing it for all of you, and it doesn't
seem hard to me. But Shakyamuni Buddha says it is difficult. Ultimately, whether it is hard or not, we still
have to speak it. I will speak whether or not you listen, too!

IF ONE UPHELD EIGHTY-FOUR THOUSAND/ DHARMA TREASUR-
IES/ AND THE TWELVE DIVISIONS OF THE CANON/ EXPOUNDING
UPON THEM TO OTHERS/ If you were to uphold all the eighty-
four thousand Dharma-doors taught by the Buddha... The
Twelve Divisions of the Canon are:

1. Prose,

2. Verse,

3. The transmitting of predictions,

4. Interjections,

5. Dharma spoken without request,

6. Causes and conditions,

7. Analogies,

8. Expanded (Vaipulya) texts,

9. Stories of the past lives of Buddhas,

10. Stories of the past lives of Disciples,

11. Previously inexistent teachings,

12. Commentarial literature.

CAUSING ALL THE LISTENERS/ TO GAIN THE SIX SPIRITUAL PENETRATIONS/: the heavenly eye, the heavenly ear, the knowledge of other's thoughts, the knowledge of past lives, the extinction of outflows, and the complete spirit. EVEN IF ONE COULD DO THIS/ IT WOULD NOT BE DIFFICULT/ BUT IF AFTER MY EXTINCTION/ ONE CAN LISTEN TO AND ACCEPT THIS SUTRA/ AND INQUIRE INTO ITS MEANING/ THAT IS DIFFICULT/ You should all think it over. It's very rare, this opportunity you now have to listen to The Dharma Flower Sutra. Don't let it slip by. Didn't I tell you before we even reached this portion of text how hard it is to hear this Sutra? It's stated very clearly here. To say nothing of how rare it is for common people like us to hear the Sutra, when Shakyamuni Buddha spoke this Sutra on Vulture Peak, even Shakyamuni Buddha's division bodies and Many Jewels Buddha came to hear it.   If, in one lifetime, you are able to hear The Dharma Flower Sutra once, in the future your wisdom will be inconceivable. Why are you so dumb now? Why are you so angry all all the time and obstructed and tormented by false think-

ing? Because you never heard The Dharma Flower Sutra.
Or perhaps you only heard one or two lectures and missed
the rest. So now you have many obstacles. You should
think, "This time I am not going to miss a single lecture!" Attend every single lecture. "If I understand
it, I'll come and listen, and if I don't understand it,
I will still come and listen. If I do understand it,
it won't hurt to deepen my understanding. If I don't
understand it, I am certainly going to find a way to
understand it." Don't miss this chance. It's worth
more than a million pounds of gold!

IF ONE WERE TO SPEAK THE DHARMA/ AND CAUSE A
THOUSAND MYRIADS OF MILLIONS/ OF LIMITLESS, COUNTLESS/
BEINGS, LIKE THE GANGES' SANDS/ TO OBTAIN ARHATSHIP/ to
certify to the fourth stage of Arhatship and obtain
patience with the non-production of dharmas, AND PER-
FECT THE SIX SPIRITUAL PENETRATIONS/ ALTHOUGH IT WOULD
BE BENEFICIAL/ IT WOULD NOT BE DIFFICULT/ BUT AFTER MY
EXTINCTION/ IF ONE CAN REVERENTLY UPHOLD/ The Dharma
Flower Sutra, SUCH A SUTRA AS THIS/ THAT INDEED IS DIF-
FICULT/ very, very difficult.

Sutra: T. 34 b 10
  I, for the sake of the Buddha Way,
  Throughout limitless lands,
  From the beginning until now,

*Have broadly expounded all the sutras
And among them all
This sutra is foremost.
If one can uphold it
He then upholds the Buddha's body.*

Outline:

>13. Explaining the dif-
>
>ficulty of upholding the
>
>Sutra.

Commentary:

Shakyamuni Buddha says, I, FOR THE SAKE OF THE
BUDDHA WAY/ in order to teach and transform living be-
ings so we can all realize the Buddha Way together,
THROUGHOUT LIMITLESS LANDS/ FROM THE BEGINNING UNTIL
NOW/ HAVE BROADLY EXPOUNDED ALL THE SUTRAS/ I lectured
on the Avatamsaka Sutra, I lectured the Agamas, the Vai-
pulya, and Prajna Sutras. Now I am lecturing The Dharma
Flower Sutra. Now I am lecturing The Dharma Flower Sutra.
AND AMONG THEM ALL/ among all the Sutras I have spoken,
THIS SUTRA IS FOREMOST/ The Dharma Flower is number one.
It is the rarest, the hardest to encounter, and the hard-
est to understand.

IF ONE CAN UPHOLD IT/ HE THEN UPHOLDS THE BUDDHA'S
BODY/ He accepts and upholds the Buddha's true body.
The Buddha's real body is within The Dharma Flower Sutra.

This is to enter the Thus Come One's room, put on the Thus Come One's robes, and sit on the Thus Come One's throne. This means that one receives and upholds the genuine body of the Buddha.

Sutra : T. 34 b 13

> Good men,
> After my extinction,
> Who can receive and uphold,
> Read, and recite this sutra,
> Now, in the presence of the Buddhas
>   should make a vow.

Outline:

> H2. Shakyamuni Buddha's exhortation.
>
>> I1. Searching for the person.

Commentary:

GOOD MEN/ and good women, AFTER MY EXTINCTION/ WHO CAN RECEIVE AND UPHOLD/ This means to recite the Sutra every day. It means to be able to recite it by heart. This doesn't mean for just one day, but every day, and every month, and every year. It doesn't mean for just one life, but in every life. No matter what we do, we must persevere. You must finish what you

1778

start. From the beginning to end, you should finish it.
You can't just uphold the Sutra one day and forget it
the next. You must make a vow to uphold The Dharma
Flower Sutra every day, month, and year, and even in
every life, life after life. READ AND RECITE THIS SUTRA/
Who can make this vow? NOW IN THE PRESENCE OF THE BUD-
DHAS/ Me and Shakyamuni Buddha,   SHOULD MAKE A VOW/
The time has come!

Sutra: T. 34 b 15
    This sutra is hard to uphold,
    If one upholds it for but an instant,
    I will rejoice,
    And so will all the Buddhas.

Outline:

12. Showing how the Bud-
dha's rejoice when one can
uphold that which is dif-
ficult to uphold.

Commentary:

THIS SUTRA IS HARD TO UPHOLD/ This Sutra is extremely difficult to uphold. If one doesn't have genuine
good roots, one will be unable to maintain it. IF ONE
UPHOLDS IT FOR BUT AN INSTANT/ In this life, if one can
maintain it... We don't know about previous lives or
future lives, but if one can uphold it in this present

life, then I WILL REJOICE/ I will be delighted with
this person. AND SO WILL ALL THE BUDDHAS/ of the ten
directions.

Sutra: T. 34 b 16
   One such as this
   Shall be praised by all the Buddhas:
   "This is courage!
   This is vigor,
   This is called morality
   And the practice of the dhutas."
   He will then quickly obtain
   The supreme Buddha Way.
   If, in the future, one
   Can read and uphold this sutra,
   He is then a true disciple of the Buddha,
   Dwelling in the pure, good stage.
   And one who after the Buddha's extinction,
   Can understand its meaning,
   Will act as eyes
   For all gods and humans in the world.
   In the age of terror,
   One who can speak it for an instant,
   Will be worthy of the offerings
   Of all the gods and humans.

Outline:

> I3. The accomplishment of
> one's own practice and
> teaching others.

Commentary:

ONE SUCH AS THIS/ who can accept and maintain The
Dharma Flower Sutra for even a moment, SHALL BE PRAISED
BY ALL THE BUDDHAS:/ They will say,"THIS IS COURAGE!/
THIS IS VIGOR/ THIS IS CALLED MORALITY/ AND THE PRACTICE
OF THE DHUTAS"/ Dhuta is a Sanskrit word which means
"striking up one's spirits." It refers to the twelve
ascetic practices. Such a one is never lazy, but works
diligently from morning until night, without feeling
tired or wanting to sleep.

HE WILL THEN QUICKLY OBTAIN/ THE SUPREME BUDDHA
WAY/ There is no position higher than that of Buddha-
hood. IF, IN THE FUTURE, ONE/ CAN READ AND UPHOLD THIS
SUTRA/ HE IS THEN A TRUE DISCIPLE OF THE BUDDHA/ DWEL-
LING IN THE PURE, GOOD STAGE/ the best place, the level
of complete goodness. AND ONE WHO, AFTER THE BUDDHA'S
EXTINCTION/ CAN UNDERSTAND ITS MEANING/ the purport of
The Dharma Flower Sutra, WILL ACT AS EYES/ FOR ALL GODS
AND HUMANS IN THE WORLD/ If there is no one upholding
The Dharma Flower Sutra, then it is like the gods and
humans are all blind. The one who upholds the Sutra func-
tions as eyes for them.

IN THE AGE OF TERROR/ that is now, in the age of

the five turbidities, ONE WHO CAN SPEAK IT FOR AN INSTANT/ WILL BE WORTHY OF THE OFFERINGS/ OF ALL THE GODS AND HU-MANS/ The Dharma Master who upholds The Dharma Flower Sutra will be worthy of offerings from people and gods.

INDEX

The Buddhist Text Translation Society:

Chairperson: Venerable Tripitaka Master Hsuan Hua, Abbot of
Gold Mountain Monastery and Tathagata Monastery,
Chancellor of Dharma Realm Buddhist University,
Professor of the Tripitaka and of the Dhyanas.

PRIMARY TRANSLATING COMMITTEE:

Chairpersons: Bhikshuni Heng Yin
Bhikshuni Heng Ch'ih

Members:

Bhikshu Heng Kuan	Bhikshuni Heng Hsien
Bhikshu Heng Sure	Bhikshuni Heng Ch'ing
Bhikshu Heng Shun	Bhikshuni Heng Hua
Bhikshu Heng Tso	Bhikshuni Heng Chen
Bhikshu Heng Teng	Bhikshuni Heng Chu
Bhikshu Heng Kung	Bhikshuni Heng Ming
Bhikshu Heng Ch'i	Bhikshuni Heng Chai
Bhikshu Heng Wu	Bhikshuni Heng Wen
	Bhikshuni Heng Tao
	Shramanerika Heng Tsai
	Shramanerika Heng Duan

Upasaka Kuo Jung (R.B.) Epstein
Upasika Kuo Ts'an (Terri) Nicholson
Upasaka Kuo Chou (David) Rounds
Upasaka Chou Kuo Li

REVIEWING COMMITTEE:

Chairpersons: Bhikshu Heng Tso
Upasaka Kuo Jung (R.B.) Epstein

Members:

Bhikshu Heng Teng	Bhikshuni Heng Yin
Bhikshu Heng Sure	Bhikshuni Heng Ch'ih
Bhikshu Heng Teng	Bhikshuni Heng Hsien
Bhikshu Heng Ch'i	Bhikshuni Heng Ch'ing
Bhikshu Heng Kung	Bhikshuni Heng Hua
	Bhikshuni Heng Chen
	Bhikshuni Heng Wen
	Bhikshuni Heng Tao
	Shramanerika Heng Tsai
	Shramanerika Heng Duan

continued on next page

Upasika Hsien Ping-ying
Upasika Kuo Ts'an Nicholson
Upasika Phuong Kuo Wu
Upasika Kuo Chin (Janet) Vickers
Upasika Kuo Han (Yao-sen) Epstein
Upasaka Kuo Chou Rounds
Upasaka Chou Kuo Li

EDITING COMMITTEE:

Chairperson: Bhikshu Heng Kuan

Members:

Bhikshu Heng Sure	Bhikshuni Heng Yin
Bhikshu Heng Lai	Bhikshuni Heng Ch'ih
Bhikshu Heng Shun	Bhikshuni Heng Hsien
Bhikshu Heng Ch'au·	Bhikshuni Heng Ch'ing
Bhikshu Heng Ch'i	Bhikshuni Heng Chu
	Bhikshuni Heng Hua
	Bhikshuni Heng Chen
	Bhikshuni Heng Jieh
	Bhikshuni Heng Ming
	Bhikshuni Heng Tao

Upasaka Kuo Jung Epstein
Upasaka Kuo Tsun (Randall) Dinwiddie
Upasika Kuo Shun (Theresa) Nolan
Upasika Kuo Ts'ai (Susan) Rounds
Upasika Kuo Ts'ung (Kathy) Dinwiddie
Upasika Kuo Chin Vickers
Upasika Kuo Ts'an Nicholson
Upasaka Kuo Chou Rounds
Upasika Kuo Lin (Nancy) Lethcoe
Upasaka Chou Kuo Li
Upasaka Yü Kuo K'ung

CERTIFYING COMMITTEE:

Chairperson: Venerable Tripitaka Master Hsuan Hua

Members:

Bhikshu Heng Kuan	Bhikshuni Heng Yin
Bhikshu Heng Sure	Bhikshuni Heng Ch'ih
Bhikshu Heng Tso	Bhikshuni Heng Hsien
	Bhikshuni Heng Ch'ing
	Bhikshuni Heng Tao

Upasaka Wong Kuo-chun
Upasaka Kuo Jung Epstein
Upasika Kuo Ts'an Nicholson
Upasika Kuo Chin Vickers

Publications from the
Buddhist Text Translation Society

All BTTS translations include extensive inter-linear commentary by the Venerable Tripitaka Master Hsuan Hua unless otherwise noted. All works available in softcover only unless otherwise noted.
ISBN Prefix: 0-917512

SUTRAS (Scriptures spoken by the Buddha):

AMITABHA SUTRA - This Sutra, which was spoken by the Buddha without being formally requested as in other Sutras, explains the causes and circumstances for rebirth in the Land of Ultimate Bliss of Amitabha (Limitless Light) Buddha. The commentary contains extensive information on common Buddhist terminology, and stories on many of the Buddha's foremost disciples. 01-4, 204 pgs., $8. (Also available in Spanish. $8.)

DHARANI SUTRA - This Sutra tells of the past events in the life of the Bodhisattva of great compassion Avalokiteshvara (Kuan Yin), and the various ways of practicing the Great Compassion Mantra, and its many benefits. It is a fundamental Secret School method. The second half of the publication is divided up into three sections. The first explains the meaning of the mantra line by line. The second has Chinese poems and drawings of division bodies of Kuan Yin for each of the 84 lines of the mantra. The last section contains drawings and verses in English on each of the 42 Hands and Eyes of Kuan Yin. This is the first English translation of this scripture. 13-8, 352 pgs., $12.

千手千眼大悲心陀羅尼經 all of the material noted above for the DHARANI SUTRA, except the commentary and the section explaining the meaning of the mantra. All the material is in Chinese only. 210 p., $6.00.

DHARMA FLOWER (LOTUS) SUTRA - In this Sutra, which was spoken in the last period of the Buddha's teaching, the Buddha proclaims the ultimate principles of the Dharma which unites all previous teachings into one. When completed the entire Sutra will be from 15 to 20 volumes. The following are those volumes which have been published to date:

VOL. I, INTRODUCTION. Discusses the Five Periods and Eight Teachings of the T'ien T'ai School and then analyzes the School's Fivefold Profound Meanings as they relate to the Sutra. The last portion introduces Tripitaka Master Kumarajiva, who translated the Sutra from Sanskrit to Chinese. 85 p., 16-2,$3.95.

VOL. II, INTRODUCTION, CHAPTER ONE. This describes the setting for the speaking of the Sutra, which includes the nature of the assembly who gathered to hear it, the Buddha's emitting of light, the questioning of Maitreya Bodhisattva, and the response from Maitreya Bodhisattva. 324 p., 22-7, $7.95.

VOL. III, EXPEDIENT METHODS, CHAPTER TWO. After the Buddha emerges from samadhi he speaks. The Buddha's foremost Arhat disciple in wisdom, Shariputra, requests the Buddha to speak further. After being requested three times the Buddha proclaims for the first time that all living beings have the potential to become Buddhas. 183 p., 26-X, $7.95.

VOL. IV, A PARABLE, CHAPTER THREE. The Buddha explains the nature of his teaching by means of an analogy of an elder who tries to rescue his five hundred children who are absorbed in their play in a burning house. 371 p., 62-6, $8.95.

VOL. V, BELIEF AND UNDERSTANDING, CHAPTER FOUR. Four of the Buddha's foremost Arhat disciples tell a story similar to the Bible's prodigal son, to express their happiness upon hearing that they too could become Buddhas in the future. 200 p., 64-2, $6.95.

VOL. VI, MEDICINAL HERBS, CHAPTER FIVE, and CONFERRING PREDICTIONS, CHAPTER SIX. In these chapters the Buddha uses the analogy of a rain-cloud to illustrate how his teaching benefits all beings with total impartiality, and he also predicts that the previously mentioned Arhat disciples will become Buddhas in the future. In bestowing his prediction he tells what their future Buddha name will be, as well as the name of their world system and kalpa, and the scope of their Dharma. 161 p., 65-0, $6.95.

VOL. VII, PARABLE OF THE TRANSFORMATION CITY, CHAPTER SEVEN. In this volume the Buddha teaches that the at-

tainment of his Arhat disciples is like a transformation city which he conjured up as an expedient when
they became weary with the journey to becoming Buddhas.
250 p., $7.95.

*VOL. VIII, FIVE HUNDRED DISCIPLES RECEIVE PREDICTIONS,
CHAPTER EIGHT, and BESTOWING PREDICTIONS UPON THOSE
STUDYING AND BEYOND STUDY, CHAPTER NINE.* More than a
thousand followers receive predictions that they will
become Buddhas in the future. 160 p., 71-5, $6.95.

VOL. IX, THE DHARMA MASTER, CHAPTER TEN. This volume
is now in preparation and will be available soon.

Other volumes of the *DHARMA FLOWER SUTRA* forthcoming.

FLOWER ADORNMENT (AVATAMSAKA) SUTRA VERSE PREFACE
清涼國師 華嚴經序淺釋), a succinct verse commentary
by T'ang Dynasty National Master Ch'ing Liang (the
Master of seven emperors), which gives a complete over-
view of all the fundamental principles contained in the
Sutra in eloquent style. First English translation.
BI-LINGUAL EDITION Chinese & English. 244 p., 28-6, $7.00.

FLOWER ADORNMENT SUTRA PROLOGUE. A detailed explanation
of the principles of the Sutra utilizing the Hsien Shou
method of analyzing scriptures known as the Ten Doors,
by National Master Ch'ing Liang. Will be approximately
5 to 10 volumes upon completion. The following volumes
have been published to date:

   *THE FIRST DOOR: THE CAUSES AND CONDITIONS FOR THE
   ARISAL OF THE TEACHING.* 252 p., 66-9, $10.00.

   *THE SECOND DOOR, PART ONE: THE STORES AND TEACHINGS
   TO WHICH IT BELONGS.* 280 p., 73-1, $10.00.

   THE SECOND DOOR, PART TWO, is now in preparation
   and will be available soon.

Other volumes of the *PROLOGUE* are forthcoming.

清深國師 華嚴經疏淺釋   , entirety of the *AVATAMSAKA
SUTRA PROLOGUE,* from First to Tenth Door, together with
interlinear commentary by Ven. Abbot Hua in four Volumes. CHINESE. $5.00, $8.50, $8.50, & $5.00.

FLOWER ADORNMENT SUTRA. Known as the king of kings of all
Buddhist scriptures because of its great length, (81 rolls
containing more than 700,000 Chinese characters) and its
profundity, it contains the most complete explanation of
the Buddha's state and the Bodhisattva's quest for Awakening. When completed the entire Sutra text with commentary
is estimated to be from 75 to 100 volumes. The following
are those volumes which have been published to date:

TEN GROUNDS, CHAPTER 26, PART 1. Contains the First
Ground of Happiness, which focuses on the practice of
giving. BILINGUAL EDITION, Chinese and English.
234 p., $7.00.

TEN GROUNDS, CHAPTER 26, PART 2. Contains the Second
Ground of Leaving Filth, the Third Ground of Emitting
Light, and the Fourth Ground of Blazing Wisdom. Eng-
lish only. 185 p., 74-x, $7.00.

Other volumes of the TEN GROUNDS CHAPTER are forthcoming.

華嚴經十地品淺釋 The Second to the Tenth Grounds,
contains the Bodhisattva's successive certification to
each of the Sagely Grounds. CHINESE only. Grounds
Two to Five in one volume now available; remaining
Grounds forthcoming.

ENTERING THE DHARMA REALM, CHAPTER 39. This chapter,
which makes up one quarter of the entire Sutra, contains
the spiritual journey of the Youth Good Wealth in his
search for Ultimate Awakening. In his quest he meets
fifty-three "Good Teachers," each of whom represents
a successive stage on the Bodhisattva path. This is
the first English translation of this chapter in its
entirety, and will comprise approximately 10 volumes
when complete. The following volumes have been published to date:

PART 1. Describes the setting for the Youth's
quest, and his meeting with Manjushri Bodhisattva.
280 p., 68-5, $8.50.

PART 2. In this volume Good Wealth meets his first
ten teachers, who represent the positions of the Ten
Dwellings. 314 p., 70-7, $8.50.

PART 3. In this volume Good Wealth is taught by the ten teachers who correspond to the levels of the Ten Conducts. 250 p., 73-1, $8.50.

PART 4. The Youth Good Wealth is taught by the ten teachers representing the Ten Transferences in the Bodhisattva stages. 173 p., 77-4.

PART 5. Good Wealth is taught by teachers who represent the Ten Bodhisattva Grounds. Now in preparation and will be available soon.

Other volumes of ENTERING THE DHARMA REALM are forthcoming, and many other chapters of the FLOWER ADORNMENT SUTRA are near publication and will be available soon.

HEART SUTRA AND VERSES WITHOUT A STAND. The text explains the meaning of Prajna Paramita, the perfection of wisdom. Each line in the Sutra is accompanied by an eloquent verse by the Ven. Abbot Hua. 155 p., 28-7, $7.50.

般若波羅蜜多心經非台頌解 , same as above, including the commentary. IN CHINESE. 120 p., $5.00.

SHURANGAMA SUTRA. This Sutra provides the most detailed explanation of the Buddha's psychology. It includes an analysis of the mind, twenty-five enlightened sages tell how they became awakened, the origin of the cosmos, the specific workings of karma, all the realms of existence, the 50 kinds of deviant samadhi-concentrations which can delude us in our search for enlightenment, and many other important principles in the Dharma. When completed, the entire Sutra will include about 10 volumes. The following volumes are Available Now.

VOL. I. The Venerable Ananda presents seven ideas on the location of the mind, and the Buddha shows how each one is incorrect and then explains the roots of the false and the true. 289 p., 17-0, $8.50.

VOL. II. The Buddha explains individual and collective karma, and reveals the true mind by showing ten different aspects of the seeing-nature. 212 p., 25-1, $8.50.

VOL. III. The Buddha gives a clear description of the qualities of all the sense-fields, their respective consciousnesses, and all of the internal and external elemental forces of the universe. He explains how all are ultimately unreal, neither existing through causes or arising spontaneously. 240 p., $8.50.

VOL. IV. In This volume the Buddha talks about the formation of the world, the coming into being of sentient creatures, and the cycle of karmic retribution in great detail. 200 p., $8.50.

VOL. V. In this volume twenty-five Sages explain the method they each used to transcend the realm of birth and death. Of them, Manjushri Bodhisattva selects the method used by the Bodhisattva Kuan Yin of "returning the hearing to listen to the Self-Nature" as the most appropriate for people in our world system. 250 p., $8.50.

VOL. VI. This volume explains the Four Clear Unalterable Instructions on Purity, and describes the Platform for and recitation of the Shurangama Mantra and its benefits. Available very soon.

Other volumes of the *SHURANGAMA SUTRA* forthcoming.

SIXTH PATRIARCH'S SUTRA. One of the foremost scriptures of Ch'an (Zen) Buddhism, this text describes the life and teachings of the remarkable Patriarch of the T'ang Dynasty, Great Master Hui Neng who, though unable to read or write, was enlightened to the true nature of all things. 235 p., 19-7, $10.00. Hardcover, $15.00.

SUTRA IN FORTY-TWO SECTIONS. In this Sutra, which was the first to be transported from India and translated into Chinese, the Buddha gives the most essential instructions in cultivating the Dharma, emphasizing the cardinal virtues of renunciation, contentment, and patience. 114 p., 15-4, $4.00.

SUTRA OF THE PAST VOWS OF EARTH STORE BODHISATTVA. This Sutra tells how Earth Store Bodhisattva attained his position as one of the greatest Bodhisattvas, foremost in vows, and also describes the workings of karma, how beings un-

dergo rebirth, and the various kinds of hells. This is
the first English translation. Hardcover only, 235 p.,
09-X, $16.00.

VAJRA PRAJNA PARAMITA (DIAMOND) SUTRA. One of the most
popular scriptures, the *VAJRA SUTRA* explains how the Bodhisattva relies on the Perfection of Wisdom to teach and
transform beings. 192 p., 02-2, $8.00.

COMMENTARIAL LITERATURE:

BUDDHA ROOT FARM. A collection of lectures given during
an Amitabha-Buddha recitation session which explains
practice and philosophy of the Pure Land School. The
instructions are very complete, especially useful for
the beginner. 72 p., 08-1, $4.00.

CITY OF TEN THOUSAND BUDDHAS DAILY RECITATION HANDBOOK
萬佛城日誦儀規 contains all the material covered in the
traditional morning, afternoon, and evening services and
special services, recited daily in Buddhist monasteries
in both East and West. Includes scriptures, praises,
chants, mantras, repentances, and so forth. BI-LINGUAL .
Chinese and English, 175 p., $8.00.

LISTEN TO YOURSELF, THINK IT OVER. The first third of
this book is instruction on how to practice the method
of reciting the name of the Bodhisattva of Great Compassion, Avalokiteshvara (Kuan Yin). The last portion
gives a very straightforward explanation of how to cultivate Ch'an (Zen) meditation. All instructions were
given during actual meditation sessions. 153 p., 24-3,
$7.00.

PURE LAND AND CH'AN DHARMA TALKS. Instructions given
during an Amitabha Buddha recitation and Ch'an meditation session, providing the essentials of each of these
most popular methods of Buddhist practice. 72 p., 08-1,
$4.00.

SHRAMANERA VINAYA AND RULES OF DEPORTMENT. The Buddha
instructed his disciples to take the Vinaya (monastic
moral code), as their teacher once he himself had en-

tered Nirvana. This text, by Great Master Lien Ch'ih
of the Ming Dynasty, explains the moral code for Shra-
maneras (novice monks). 112 p., 04-9, $4.00.

緇門崇行錄, An ancient text compiled by Great Master Lien Ch'ih of the Ming Dynasty, on the Vinaya (moral code) for Bhikshus. No commentary. CHINESE. 130 p.

SHURANGAMA MANTRA COMMENTARY. An ancient text explaining
how to practice the foremost mantra in the Buddha's teaching, including a line by line analysis of the mantra. The
first volume contains all the instructions on how to pre-
pare before holding the mantra, and an explanation of the
first portion of the mantra. BILINGUAL, Chinese and English. To appear in many volumes. Volume Two available
very soon.

SONG OF ENLIGHTENMENT. The lyric poem of the state of
the Ch'an sage, by T'ang Dynasty Master Yung Chia.
AVAILABLE SOON.

永嘉大師證道歌詮釋, same as above with commentary
by the Ven. Abbot Hua. CHINESE. 40 p., $2.50.

宣化上人偈讚闡釋錄, Verses by the Ven. Abbot Hua.
IN CHINESE. 73 p., $5.00.

THE TEN DHARMA REALMS ARE NOT BEYOND A SINGLE THOUGHT.
An eloquent poem on all the realms of being, which is accompanied by extensive commentarial material and drawings.
72 p., 12-X, $4.00.

BIOGRAPHICAL:

RECORDS OF THE LIFE OF THE VENERABLE MASTER HSUAN HUA.
The life and teachings of the Ven. Abbot from his birth-
place in China, to the present time in America.
   VOL. I, covers the Abbot's life in China. 96 p.,
   07-3, $5.00. ALSO IN SPANISH, $8.00.
   VOL. II, covers the events of the Abbot's life as he
   cultivated and taught his followers in Hong Kong.
   This volume contains many photos, poems and stories.
   229 p., 10-3, $8.00.

宣化 禅師事蹟, same as above Volumes I and II.
IN CHINESE. 94 p., $6.00.

THREE STEPS, ONE BOW. The daily journal of American
Bhikshus Heng Ju and Heng Yo, who in 1973-74 made a
religious pilgrimage from Gold Mountain Monastery in
San Francisco to Marblemount, Washington, bowing every
third step on their way. The pilgrimage was inspired
by the conduct of ancient monks in China, who would bow
every third step for thousands of miles to famous monasteries or renowned teachers. 160 p., 1809, $5.95.

WORLD PEACE GATHERING. A collection of instructional
talks on Buddhism commemorating the successful completion
of the bowing pilgrimage of Bhikshus Heng Ju and Heng
Yo. 128 p., 05-7, $5.00.

WITH ONE HEART BOWING TO THE CITY OF 10,000 BUDDHAS. The
moving journals of American Bhikshus Heng Sure and Heng
Ch'au, who make a "three steps, one bow" pilgrimage from
Gold Wheel Temple in Los Angeles to the City of 10,000
Buddhas, located 110 miles north of San Francisco.

   VOL. I, May 6 - June 30, 1977, 180 p., 21-9, $6.00.
   VOL. II, July 1 - October 30, 1977, 322 p., 23-5, $7.50.
   VOL. III, October 30 - December 16, 1977, 154 p., $6.00.
   VOL. IV, December 17, 1977 - January 21, 1978, 130 p.,
          $6.00.
   VOL. V, January 22-February 18, 1978, 127 p., $5.00.

   VOL. VI. Available very soon.

   Other volumes to appear in sequence, including the
journals from the continuation of "Three Steps One Bow"
within the City of 10,000 Buddhas still in progress to
date.

修行者的消息 - *NEWS FROM TWO CULTIVATORS - LETTERS OF
THREE STEPS, ONE BOW.* The letters from Dharma Masters
Heng Sure and Heng Ch'au chronicling the entirety of
their 2 1/2 year journey to reach the City of 10,000 Buddhas. CHINESE only. $7.00.

HENG CH'AU'S JOURNAL. An account of the remarkable exper-
iences and changes undergone by Bhikshu Heng Ch'au when he
first came in contact with Gold Mountain Monastery.
24 p., $1.95.

OPEN YOUR EYES, TAKE A LOOK AT THE WORLD. The journals of Bhikshus Heng Sure and Heng Ch'au and Bhikshuni Heng Tao, taken during the 1978 Asia-region visit by the Ven. Abbot Hua together with other members of the Sino-American Buddhist Association. 347 p., 32-4, $7.50.

放眼觀世界--亞州弘法記 ,
the above in Chinese,
347 p., $7.50.

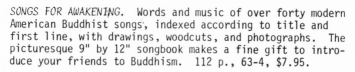

MUSIC, NOVELS, AND BROCHURES:

SONGS FOR AWAKENING. Words and music of over forty modern American Buddhist songs, indexed according to title and first line, with drawings, woodcuts, and photographs. The picturesque 9" by 12" songbook makes a fine gift to introduce your friends to Buddhism. 112 p., 63-4, $7.95.

AWAKENING. A 12" stereo record album of ten Buddhist songs in Western style (all in English) ranging from pop to rock, to folk and country. Subjects covered include: Bodhisattva vows, the *Book of Changes,* Ch'an meditation, Lao-tzu, the *Lotus Sutra,* Abhidharma meditations, Amitabha Buddha and his Pure Land, and more. The album includes a full lyric sheet, a printed insert of Chinese translation, and linear notes clarifying concepts and sources. $7.00. Also available in casette tape, $7.00.*

   Forthcoming soon:

   THREE CART PATRIARCH. A 12" stereo LP recorded by and for children, based on the Monkey Tales of China, featuring story, six sparkling musical productions, and many special features. $7.00.*

   HEART LIKE GLUE and other songs on an EP by Bhiksuni Heng Yin & the Wondrousound Band.*

   BENEFITTING OTHERS (what you do after "Awakening"). 12" stereo LP of Buddhist songs currently in progress.*

*All record and tape orders should be sent to: Wondrous Sound Music, City of 10,000 Buddhas, P.O. Box 217 Talmage, CA 95481. Tel. (707) 462-0939.

POSTAGE AND HANDLING:

United States: $1.00 for the first book and 40¢ for each additional book. All publications are sent via special fourth class. Allow from 4 days to 2 weeks for delivery.

International: $1.25 for the first book and 75¢ for each additional book. All publications are sent via "book rate." We recommend that for orders of approximately 10 or more, an additional $3.00 per parcel of 10 books be sent for registration to protect against loss. We are not responsible for parcels lost in the mail.

All orders require pre-payment before they will be processed.

Send all orders to:

Buddhist Text Translation Society
Gold Mountain Monastery
1731 Fifteenth Street
San Francisco, CA 94103, U.S.A.

The City of Ten Thousand Buddhas is the headquarters and main center of the Sino-American Buddhist Association. In addition to a rigorous daily schedule of work, study, translation, and cultivation, the City sponsers various meditation and study programs throughout the year. Under the auspices of Dharma Realm Buddhist University, the City also offers a wide array of courses on Buddhist subjects, languages, and the arts. If you would like more information on the programs at the City of 10,000 Buddhas, you may write to:

City of Ten Thousand Buddhas
Talmage, CA 95481, U.S.A.
Tel: (707) 462-0939